TUESDAY IN TEXAS

Growing Up in Texas in the '50s

Rebecca Long Hayden

TNT Publications

ALEXANDRIA, VIRGINIA

Rebecca Long Hayden/TNT Publications
5901 Mt Eagle Drive, #118
Alexandria, Virginia 22303
www.website-url.com

Cover Design by Leslie Leonard
Book Layout © 2014 BookDesignTemplates.com

Tuesday in Texas/ Rebecca Long Hayden. -- 1st ed.
ISBN 1519-352484

This memoir is fondly dedicated to
The Texas City High School Graduating Class of 1964.

The life of a person is not what happened, but what he remembers and how he remembers it.

—GABRIEL GARCIA MARQUEZ

CONTENTS

Requesting the Pleasure of your Company

1. Members of the Class of '64 in 2006.

The Texas City High School Graduating Class of 1964 has mystically reinvented itself as we should have been, and not as we were, all in the name of second chances. A few generous leaders sent out an invitation: Come to the reunion! Come back and be welcome, popular kids, band kids, fringe kids, cowboys, and hoods. Come be part of the class in our wisdom and maturity. Remember as you will what was small and exclusive, but come back and be welcome now. The quote of this introduction, although penned by Marquez, was passed along by an outstanding member of our class, Linda Cooper, and within this context, it seems particularly appropriate.

The very word *memory* evokes a visceral response – deep in the heart, in the mind, in a singular place, different in all of us. There's a barren patch between fact and fiction, a place where we toss out seeds and something grows, something made of memory and truth. Why do we remember things a certain way? Why does someone who shared the same experience remember it so differently? Memory has much to do with truth and little to do with fact, and as for fact? As time goes by I trust that word less and less.

2. Linda Cooper

I began this memoir to satisfy my creative need, which pesters like a tune stuck in my head. If you have it, you know what I mean. Write something! Paint something! Build something! But would anyone be interested in stories about me?

As I began to write, the main character surfaced, and it wasn't me after all. The main character was a time and place. Growing up in Texas in the 1950s – that's the story, and I'm a minor player, a narrator if you will, either reliable or unreliable. The reader will be the judge of that.

The '40s? The '50s? Where's the tipping point? Change doesn't line up neatly by decade. The Class of 2002 would say the cataclysm happened on September 11, 2001, when the twin towers of the World Trade Center thundered down, and a different America emerged from the noise. For the Class of 1942, it was December 7, 1941, at Pearl Harbor.

For children of the '50s, the pivot happened on November 22, 1963. In 1961 President John F. Kennedy inspired *a new generation of Americans—born in this century, tempered by war, disciplined by a hard and bitter peace, proud of our ancient heritage . . .*

For anyone who grew up in that era, that's who we were when we entered high school. Then in November of 1963 JFK was dead, his head blown apart by a sniper's bullet. Even though it was 1963, *the '60s* in context refers to the late '60s – the ramping up of the Vietnam war, the passage of the Civil Rights Act, the second wave of feminism. The '50s died with President Kennedy.

I remember the moment when Mrs. Mary Agnes Neyland, the English teacher, left the room at a knock on the door, and when she returned, she stood white and silent in front of us. Teachers at Texas City High didn't lose their composure, but she allowed herself a deep breath. First, she forbade any kind of outburst. Then she told us the news from Dallas.

When the bell rang we walked into the hall shocked, not believing it could be so. We moved through the next months and on to graduation night. The Class of '64, who thought we would dance into the future, made our way with *measured steps and slow*, as Dante put it, into a different world than it was when we entered high school.

Before I request the pleasure of your company on my journey through time, allow me to warn you in advance. I have an imprudent sense of humor. I sometimes laugh at the exchange of wedding vows, giggle at gravesides, and applaud people who behave outrageously in public. A friend told me she loves me best, because when she used to drink and dance on tabletops, her other friends tried to stop her. I yelled "Go, Joyce, GO!"

And I'm not politically correct. I call things by their names, meaning no offense. I've been known to say *Indian* and even *dwarf.* (Really? *So it's Snow White and the Seven Little People*?) I would never deliberately hurt anyone, but I'm a human being, and to my regret, I have hurt people and no doubt will again, maybe in this memoir. If I do, it was never intentional and never would be.

I'll lead into the first chapter by remembering what my mother used to say when we were a long way from home. She spoke of Texas with a longing I didn't understand. Her blue eyes would mist, and she would start a story: "When we lived in Texas . . ."

One day she amended her segue. "Tuesday," she said. "We'll be back in Texas."

There shortly followed a ride in an actual taxi (my first), a cross-country bus trip, a kidnapping, and although we didn't make it by Tuesday, we did make it. We got back to her hometown of Texas City, Texas, landing in the lap of unsuspecting relatives.

I understand my mother's longing for the Lone Star State like I didn't when I was a child. I've lived elsewhere for many years, yet Texas is the geographic love of my life. It makes me happy to write about growing up there, when it was beautiful and simple.

Or is that just how I remember it?

CHAPTER ONE

Welcome to Texas City, Where It's Always Halloween

3. Texas City as I first saw it.

Late October 1955, rolling into Texas City on a Greyhound bus, this is what I saw:

A metropolis on the distant skyline, huge, beckoning, a fantasy city. I mostly lived in books, so I compared it to Oz, the Emerald City, green and glowing. This town twinkled like a Christmas tree, tiny orange lights running up the towering skyscrapers, an Amber City. We were near the coast. Were those lighthouses?

"It's so big," I said, sleepy, never sure of my mother's mental whereabouts, even though she sat right beside me on the bus.

"Not that big," she said.

"But the buildings. And lighthouses?"

"What? Oh. That's the plants."

In a symmetrical loop personal history often makes, my son at a young age told an interested adult that his dad worked in a flower shop. This was way off the mark, so I asked where he got that idea.

"Daddy's a plant manager," he said.

Perfect logic, and that remark took me right back to the night I saw Texas City for the first time. I would grow up, move away, and live in many cities, but I would call that little coastal town *home* for the rest of my life.

When I first saw it, I was nine years old. I understood the *plants* my mother referred to weren't organic things. No leaves. No green. It would sort itself out, I assumed, probably for the worse. That was my experience of life so far.

"Raymond works at Monsanto," my mother offered. "Everyone works at the plants." Raymond was the husband of my mother's older sister Jackie Benskin Morris.

My mother closed her eyes, exhausted from an ordeal that began ten years ago and culminated in this cross-country flight from a marriage that never should have happened.

The flame-tongues topped smokestacks, not lighthouses. The amber lights framed miles of pipes, gauges, tanks, and other fittings of huge oil refineries. As we drew closer to town, the buildings in the distance morphed into skeletons, like an erector set. Though I still glimpsed the lights in the distance, we were traveling through a much less impressive skyline now, and soon the bus slowed, eased into a parking lot, and the air breaks sighed us to a stop.

So this is it, I thought.

Texas City. Blown to bits in 1947, blown away in 1961 (not for the first or last time), and smelling like a giant fart at all times due to the fumes from Monsanto, Union Carbide, Amoco, and the other refineries that provided a living for the town folk, who remembered hard times. Since you never got used to going hungry, and you got used to the smell, most thought it was a good tradeoff.

Explosions? Hurricanes? What did that matter weighed against three square meals a day, every day? And a home. And a car. It was the American Dream, the opportunity for prosperity, success, and upward mobility through hard work.

My only dream that night was I might soon find a place to sleep. It was dark, and I thought it was Tuesday. My mother said we would be in Texas by Tuesday when we left New Castle, Pennsylvania. She had pulled two pre-packed suitcases out of a closet as soon as my father left to do whatever he did during the day (it wasn't work). We got in a cab, boarded a bus, and watched as the gray winter streets of town disappeared behind us. When my father discovered we were gone, he gave chase.

My mother would head to Texas City, he knew, because that's where she grew up with her parents Ruby and Charley Benskin, and her sisters Jackie and Dorothy. My grandparents had moved "up the country" years before, but Aunt Jackie had settled in TC, and she was the strong one. We would go there because that's where we could survive.

My father ambushed us somewhere in Kentucky or Indiana, sat us down in a dingy bus station diner, and did his charming best to convince my mother not to leave him. When it didn't work, he turned mean and snatched my three-year-old sister. In spite of my mother's pleas, he disappeared into the half-light of dawn or dusk, which one is unclear in my memory. I only see the fading light and my sister's black eyes, frightened, looking back over his shoulder, getting small, smaller, and then gone.

After the kidnapping, we retreated to a cheap motel while my mother tried to recover and decide what to do, which was to push on, and here we were, in a dark parking lot in Texas City.

As we waited our turn to disembark from the bus, I took advantage of the pause in forward motion to ask a question I'd been mulling over. Why did my father take my sister and leave me behind?

"She was easier to carry." When confronted with thorny problems, my mother turned either vague or practical or both. I guess it was a weighty question to both of us, but not in the same way.

I adored my mother, but even so, at times she got on

4. My Mother the Butterfly, about 1952.

my nine-year-old nerves. I might as well have a butterfly for a mother. She was lovely, small, fragile, and she gave the false impression that her existence on earth was ephemeral. If I wasn't careful, she would disappear in a puff of golden dust.

We got off the bus, and I saw a real estate office, a sign that said Bus Depot, and another sign – vertical – e above the l and so on – that said *Ellis'*.

My mother was canny about certain things, and she wanted to beat the other passengers to the phone booth. We headed straight to it, me trailing so close I slammed into her when she stopped. By the time the change trickled down the slot, there was a line behind us.

I heard only one side of the conversation. "Hello? Jackie? This is Hazel. I'm here."

I could easily imagine what Jackie said: *Hazel? Here? Here where?*

"At the bus station." She glanced at the sign. "Ellis's. Can you come get us? It's just Becky and me. I'll explain when I see you."

No telling what shape my mother was in. She had scraped together enough money to leave, had her youngest child grabbed along the way, and she had nothing but a high school education, good looks, and a sister she could count on. Few resources were available to women in those days, so this would have taken a super-human effort.

My mother backed out of the phone booth. "It's Friday night. They were going to the football game, but they're coming."

I would believe it when I saw it. I was used to being misled by adults, and by now I knew it wasn't even Tuesday. In Texas everyone knows where everyone is on fall Friday nights. At the high school

5. Ellis's Restaurant and Bus Depot. From *Images of America - Texas City*, by Albert L. Mitchell.

football game. Your kid doesn't have to play. You don't have to have a kid in school. It doesn't matter if the team hasn't won a game in 10 years.

But they did come, my Aunt Jackie, my Uncle Raymond, and my cousin Beverly. My older cousin Ray had gone on to the game. Beverly, a curious 12-year-old, perhaps was not allowed to go, or maybe she thought our arrival was more interesting than football. She told me later how the conversation went after my mother's phone call.

Aunt Jackie: *I'll bet she's left Dick.*

Uncle Raymond: *Thank God. But what will we do with them?*

Aunt Jackie: *Well, they'll have to stay here for a while.*

By the time we were in the car, my level of astonishment was hitting new peaks. It started with the non-lighthouses and ramped up

6. My cousin Ray Morris, Uncle Raymond, and Beverly by the Big Oldsmobile. It was blue and white.

over everything. The Morris's enormous Oldsmobile. The volume of Beverly's can-can slips. The mustard seed encased in glass on a gold chain around her neck. My possessions filled one small suitcase. I determined that I would get a mustard seed as soon as possible.

Looking out the car window, I was impressed. Everything was so … orderly. No twists and turns, no hills, not even trees to speak of, no Pennsylvania dusting of early snow. Just streets crossing each other on an axis. The buildings might have been made from giant shoe boxes in slightly varied sizes. In 1955 it would have been hard to name anything in Texas City that was pretty, except the sky, but even the proudest residents credited God and not the municipality for that. Still, this plainness struck me as perfect. Up until then, nothing in my life approached orderly. What a relief.

Inside the Morris home on 21st Avenue, things *were* pretty. Cared for. It was wonderful. I was installed in Beverly's room where the wonders continued. I admired her orange and black banners, cut-outs, and book covers, and I remarked on her enthusiasm for Halloween, which was only days away. She looked at me like I must be out of my mind.

"Oh." She laughed. "Orange and black. That's the

7. **Aunt Jackie and Beverly about 1954.**

high school colors. In Texas City it's always Halloween!"

I learned how true Bev's statement was, and as the kids say today, in a good way. A lot of words describe my home town in the '50s and

'60s. Wacky. Weird. Wonderful. Petty. Safe. Generous. Interesting. Fun. Just like Halloween.

I don't know a lot about the machinations of the next months. The Morris family supported us; I don't know where my mother would have gotten any money otherwise. She worked for a time at the Singer Sewing Store down on Sixth Street. Everything was down on Sixth Street – I heard that all the time. Where's the drugstore? Down on Sixth Street. Where's the movie? Down on Sixth Street.

And down on Sixth Street the Butterfly got fired because she couldn't keep her mind on her work for worrying about my stolen baby sister.

At the time I was weirdly in sync with my mother. One evening Bev and I were Christmas shopping (down on Sixth Street). I was intoxicated by the bins of colorful options in Rock's Variety Store, when suddenly I had a vision of my mother falling in front of a car. She was blocks away at Penny's, but I saw it in my head and felt her sickening fear. The car stopped, and she was unhurt, but when they told me about it, I didn't say a word. I knew it was spooky, and I knew they wouldn't believed me. Besides, I had enough to figure out, such as who were these relatives I didn't know but found myself living with?

I loved my aunt and her husband Raymond immediately. To this day, when I hear the word *decent*, they come to mind. Also *kind*. My cousin Beverly laughed a lot, and I liked that. Also, she was a girl, so we had that in common.

My cousin Ray, on the other hand, was as exotic as a purple giraffe, and he scared me for no reason except he was the first teenage boy I ever met. But he had good manners and a kind heart, so he did his best to tolerate the invasion of the Butterfly and her spawn. He was tall, good-looking, had a crew cut, and could drive a car. People called him on the phone. I never saw anything like it. He was 17. I was awed.

As for Beverly, she tolerated me with grace most of the time, especially considering I lived not only in her house, but in her room. One night after lights out, my tossing about like a mangy cat got to her. In a snit, she jumped out of bed, switched on a lamp, and rummaged in her combination desk/dressing table – you lifted the lid and there were cubbie holes in the cavity and a mirror on the back of the lid – fantastic. Among the pink lipsticks and glittery bits, she found what she was looking for, a piece of colored chalk. She drew a line down the middle of the bed, which horrified me. Defacing anything was a mortal sin in the '50s. Then she threatened me with death if ever again I crossed the line during the night.

She leaned in and lowered her voice. "I was here when the disaster happened, you know."

Bev's encounter with the grim reaper (she used that term) happened while she was picking buttercups in Snug Harbor (a neighborhood, not a harbor). She was little more than a baby on April 16, 1947, when the *S.S. Grandcamp* exploded in Texas City harbor, and the force of the blast five miles away flattened her. All hell broke loose that day. Six hundred people died, 145 at the Monsanto plant alone, but Uncle Raymond worked for Union Carbide then, so he was OK.

"Hundreds were killed," my cousin said, "all over town. Bodies everywhere. Body parts, too."

I was impressed, astonished, amazed, and after that, I woke up every morning clinging to my side of the bed.

The last member of the Morris household was Teddy the parakeet, who was allowed out of his cage to fly around at will. I never imagined such a pet, and I wondered about bird ca-ca. Aunt Jackie kept a clean house, so where did the ca-ca go?

One morning Teddy lined up with the back of my mother's head and swooped in from behind for a two-point landing. She didn't see him coming, and the explosion of tangled curls and bird talons startled her and Teddy both. She fell to the floor, and when it was over, her cup was shattered and there was coffee on all nearby surfaces. Teddy squawked frantically and worked himself loose from her hair, but his panic caused him to deliver a load of you-know-what pretty much everywhere.

The colored girl was called in, another unheard-of amazement. The Morris's had a colored girl who came sometimes, and I was to see her and my aunt on their knees scrubbing the floor. You called them *colored* to be polite, and you got your money's worth by working as hard as they did. There were no bird droppings or anything else left when they were done, and I learned something. If you want to inspire people to work hard, work hard yourself.

8. Me with my mother and my sister Tish, Easter 1956, Fourth Avenue.

Against all this newness a fresh dread arose. I heard conversations about my mother's plans to return to Pennsylvania to retrieve my sister, and after the first of the year, it happened. She left on a train, and I thought I would never see her again. Neither Aunt Jackie's gentle reassurances nor Uncle Raymond's offers of Coca-Cola could convince me she would come back. She did, and with my baby sister. Poor Morris family. Now we were multiplying.

The return of my mother was a miracle. I didn't think my father would part with Tish, and I didn't think my mother would come back

9. The Garage apartment behind Mrs. Wagner's house, 2008.
It looks almost the same as it did when I lived there.

for me. When my father snatched my sister and left me behind, I was forever consigned to the world of the less desirable, but at least with the return of my sister, my mother became functional. She found a job, and she kept it. The fact that my aunt worked outside the home was controversial – it was the era of *my wife doesn't have to work* – but they had a brand new home with a mortgage, a couple of half-grown kids, and my uncle's pay as a pipefitter, though good for the times, didn't cover all their dreams.

Ray for sure would go to college and Beverly, too, if she didn't get married first. That's how folks thought then, especially blue-collar folks, and that was Texas City. A beautiful, blue-collar town, through and through. And although Aunt Jackie spoke softly and was as pretty as my mother, my aunt didn't flit around, not ever. When her family needed extra money, she got a job.

Furthermore, her job led to my mother's job. Aunt Jackie learned that a doctor in the same building where she worked needed a receptionist. My aunt put forth my mother's name, and Dr. Leonti hired her. We moved into a garage apartment behind the Widow Wagner's house on Fourth Avenue, close enough so my mother could walk to work.

So my sister was retrieved, my mother had a job, and we moved into the garage apartment. If the Morris's were relieved, they waved us goodbye without showing it.

I had just turned 10 years old. I was officially a Texas Citian. I was home.

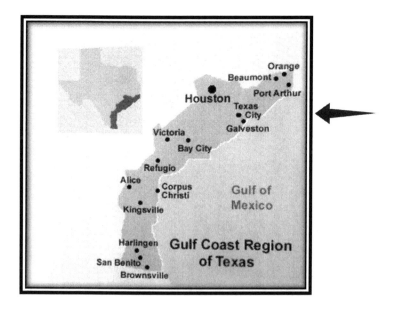

CHAPTER TWO

Ronnie Wilson Wins a Pony

Standing by my mother looking at Roosevelt-Wilson Elementary School, I saw sky. So much sky the low buildings seemed irrelevant. I didn't take to the tall trees and rolling hills of Pennsylvania, but the sky over Texas City in my memory is cast in bright blue all the time, with white clouds just for emphasis. The sky made me feel like my troubles might rise up and drift away, leaving room for whatever adventure would happen next.

10. Me about 1955.

Not too much time passed after our arrival in TC before someone thought of enrolling me in school, probably Aunt Jackie, and Roosevelt was the closest to my aunt's house, where we lived at the time.

11. Roosevelt-Wilson Elementary School. From
Images of America - Texas City, **by Albert L. Mitchell.**

As I stood outside the school staring at the sky, I smelled the chemical odor from the refineries, which I was already getting used to, but I also smelled rotting fish, old mud, and the pungent aroma of wind over salt water in Galveston Bay, only two blocks away. I liked that, though I knew it wasn't roses.

The school squatted on a piece of land so vast it seemed like a prairie, right there in the middle of town. Rows of neat houses lined the streets on both sides of the field, houses with swept sidewalks and grass lapping at the curbs. Even the children walking to school had a mowed look, scrubbed, tucked in, belted, flat-topped and pony-tailed.

There would be three marvels before the school year ended, two of kindness and another more spectacular one concerning a pony, which I'm pretty sure I imagined. But to tell about these things, I have to tell about Roosevelt-Wilson School. My friend Lana recently said that everything in Texas City seemed perfectly normal until you said it out loud, and writing about it is the same way. It all seemed normal at the time, but it was much more fun than that.

My mother's final advice as we approached the enrollment office was "be yourself." I wanted to be Zorro, Scout Finch, or Annette Funicello. I had no idea who I was or where I belonged. I wasn't even a Texan, as far as I knew.

Thanks to the research of a second cousin, I have learned that my roots go all the way back to the Republic of Texas and beyond. I wish I had known sooner, but when I arrived in Texas City I thought I was from Pennsylvania and had lived in San Antonio before that for a while. In short, I was almost an alien.

I was installed in Mrs. Schleser's fourth grade. I scrambled to catch up academically, but it wasn't too hard because I was a reading fool. I pestered for a library card as

12. John J. Long, my great great grandfather, who fought in the Army of the Republic of Texas.

soon as we arrived in TC. Pestering was effective with my mother. She gave me what I wanted if she could so I would be quiet.

I could read well because the first week of second grade a teacher in San Antonio told my mother I couldn't read a lick. My mother understood all the up-rooting was having a negative effect on my education, and this bothered her. "Sit down," she said one evening after the teacher ratted me out. My mother brought out a completely inappropriate work of popular fiction called *Forever Amber*, opened the page, and pointed a red-lacquered nail at the first word.

"Read," she said.

We did this every night for what seemed like years. We read movie magazines, comic books, newspapers, and whatever she could get her hands on, including cereal boxes and milk cartons. *Sound it out, sound it out.* To this day, when I have a problem to solve, those words echo in my head. *Sound it out.*

Soon I didn't need her encouragement. I loved to read, and I would for the rest of my life. She breathed a sigh of relief, went back to what she was doing, and I was quiet for the next ten years. I learned a lesson. Everything has an up-side. If it hurt to have my parents tell me to go away, I had a place to go – into books, and it's one of the best things that ever happened to me.

I started slow at Roosevelt, and right away my squinty eyes tipped off Mrs. Schleser. I couldn't see diddly from more than five feet out. She moved me to a front desk, but I needed glasses, and they were provided, though I don't know from where. There was a limit to my aunt's resources, if not to her generosity. Because I probably read at a college level, and now I could see what I was doing, I caught on to most things.

My clearest memory is that I was happy. Anger would surface later with regard to my father, but children trust their intuition, and mine told me the worst was over. People who have unhappy childhoods have a lot of company. Bad stuff happens. I hate clichés, but the truest one is *that's life.* You have to cope, and I coped by reading and laughing. A sense of humor is a gift, and it hasn't failed me often. My way is to laugh and stay centered. Things generally aren't rotten or perfect. They're somewhere in the middle, with a tilt one way or another from time to time.

For instance, on the way to Texas, after the great kidnapping caper occurred, we had to return to the bus for our things, and one of the passengers made me laugh, despite everything. The fellow had been with us on the bus all the way from Pittsburgh, and although I didn't know anything about sex except there were two genders, I knew when men flirted with my mother, probably because it happened pretty often. Our fellow traveler, who had tried a couple of times to chat her up, chose just that moment to take another shot.

"Hey. I thought you had two kids." He chucked me under the chin. "Did you hang on to this one because she's so cute?"

I couldn't help myself. I laughed. Not because what he said was funny, but because I was pretty sure this was an epic fail. My mother burst into tears, and I stopped laughing. We got off the bus and headed to our sinister-looking motel, and the comedian slunk away, probably to die of embarrassment before he got to Louisiana.

What did I know when I was introduced to the clean inmates of Mrs. Schleser's fourth grade? I could read. I could laugh. I had my aunt and uncle and my cousins Beverly and Ray (scary, but he was blood – kids feel the pull of that). I had my mother. As for my baby sister, I had hopes we would recover her, and we had.

The next thing I learned was that I had no talent at all for making new friends. It's a family joke that I rarely get that first bit right. My opening salvos at parties have been known to clear out whole rooms, I get it so wrong.

Once at a party my friend Jo Ann mentioned that her mother was there. In an attempt at small talk, I asked a person who looked a little like Jo if she happened to be Jo's mother. The woman turned an icy eye on me. "I'm Jo's college roommate." The conversation group dispersed. I could tell several stories like that, but one's enough to make the point.

I've known people who make friends easily, like Jeanie from high school, always surrounded by admirers. My cousin Beverly met Prince Charles when she lived in England. He made a public appearance and spoke to her in the crowd. They laughed like old friends, and he probably sends her Christmas cards. If my husband Brian is with anyone for more than ten minutes, he's got a friend.

13. Jeanie Vandaveer

This still does not happen to me, but I'm consoled because I make friends that last a lifetime. It doesn't matter if it takes time in the beginning.

Still, it was a problem when I was new in town. I was *poorly socialized*, as a shrink might put it. I arrived in TC never having had a friend. I never went to the same school for one whole year. I never went to anyone's house. I didn't know any children. The up-side: I've always known how to be content in my own company, and adjusting to change comes easy.

But about the marvels. The first was the kindness shown in the Morris home, where my aunt in particular showed her sensitivity in what she probably thought were small ways. To me, they were enormous. For instance, there was one TV set, and I don't mean one in every room, like now. I mean one TV. People had to work with that. My aunt realized the most important activity in my life besides reading was the Mickey Mouse club, and she made everyone stand down for half an hour in the afternoon so I could watch. The thought still thrills me! M-I-C-K-E-Y – pause – M-O-U-S-E. Annette. Cubby. Darlene. Every day I couldn't wait. Thank you, Aunt Jackie.

The whole time I was enrolled at Roosevelt-Wilson, I probably said a total of 10 words. I moved around like a phantom, quiet, because I didn't know I was supposed to talk. Overtures were made to me, particularly by a girl named Renee Larrey, who saw something interesting in me. She invited me to her house. I found this troubling because it had never happened before, but I went, and it was the nicest house I had ever been in. It had pillars across a front porch. I don't know how I did. OK, I guess. I knew how to be polite, and that's all the grownups of my acquaintance required. Renee moved away in junior high, but I never forgot her.

I remember Dennis, too, because he was sweet as prepubescent boys can be. When I was moved to the front of the classroom because I couldn't

14. Dennis Thompson

see, I landed next to him, and he spoke to me. I think I may have spoken back. Was I shy or aloof? No. I simply couldn't think of what to say to someone I didn't know. It's still hard for me.

One day at school a particularly bouncy person with a whistle came to the door of my class and announced: *PE*!

I didn't know what *PE* meant. Public Education? Poor Eyesight? I knew about recess, but that was way more disorganized. I lined up and was marched to the gym with all the other fourth grade girls, and that's where I met Dolores, who was so beautiful I couldn't stop staring at her. When it got warm outside we would have softball or kickball, but at that time of year it was dancing. All those little girls, including Dolores, pranced around like care-free leprechauns. I wanted to laugh from the pleasure of the sight.

Dolores talked to me, and I understood that she wasn't only pretty, she was smart and funny. After fourth grade, I didn't see her again until junior high, and by then the Big P (puberty) had descended like a fog, and everyone was loco. Still, I remembered Dolores. In junior high she was stunning and popular, and I was undistinguished. (Years later she would be among the leaders who brought the class of '64 together again.)

I was even more hindered in the friends-making arena because I was the only kid in the Texas City Independent School District who had divorced parents. This is certainly untrue, but it's what I thought. Divorce was rarer by a zillion than it is now. Better socialized kids asked me things, like where did my father work? I didn't realize this was only fourth grade small talk. They expected to hear something like Amoco, Monsanto, or down on Sixth Street at First State Bank.

15. Dolores Geaslin

My mind flew to the truth. *He's been drunk for two years, hasn't worked in three, and I have no idea where he is or what he's doing.*

I'd rather have died than say that.

So I said he was a Fuller Brush salesman. At some point he had gone from door to door selling brushes. This seemed an honorable pursuit, so I said it, with no further explanation. I probably looked so stricken any sensible kid resolved on the spot never to talk to me again.

Although I fell in love with Texas City at first sight, sometimes such things trickle away. However, the final thud of falling in love came with the two remaining marvels. The mythical one first: Ronnie Wilson won a pony at the Roosevelt-Wilson spring carnival.

My state of mind by the spring of 1956 bordered on rapture. I always get spring fever. May comes and I'm singing songs from *Camelot*, planting things that can't possibly survive in my growing zone, and thinking I'll win the lottery. Mix the anticipation of the school carnival with spring fever, plus having my mother and sister safely back from Pennsylvania, and in fourth grade I must have been like a pig-tailed tomboy on a sugar high. Sorting out what's possible about Ronnie and the pony has led me to believe I heard about the big win and embroidered the rest. If you know, don't tell me; I like my memory as it is. In my mind I see Ronnie running down 14th Avenue with a pony.

I'm sure Ronnie did win something, but in my memory, it wasn't a certificate he could take home saying he could have a pony or two-hundred dollars, so his parents could call someone and say, "Keep the pony. Send the money."

Nope. This was Texas City in 1956. When his name was drawn, they handed him the reins.

"Congratulations, kid! Here's your pony."

Can you imagine such a thing these days? Modern moms pee in their pants if a kid comes home with a goldfish. Someone has to FEED it for God's sake! Ronnie lived near Bay Street, a few blocks from the school, and he ran home with the winsome beast trotting behind. And here's how I remember Texas City moms. I'll bet his mom took it in stride.

Oh, a pony. Good for you, Ronnie. Take him around back and tie him to the tallow tree. She probably rolled her eyes when he was out of sight and started sorting out what to do, but she didn't act like someone should be sued.

The third wonder is real, though it took time for me to realize how marvelous it was.

By spring I was living on Fourth Avenue in the Danforth School District, but Mrs. Schleser was adamant I should not change schools so late in the year. Transportation was the problem, as my mother couldn't afford a car. For no reason except kindness Mrs. Schleser drove all the way across town to pick me up and take me home, every school day for the remainder of the year.

At the time, I thought this was odd, because changing schools in the middle of the year was my normal, all I'd ever known. Looking back, I see what a fine thing it was. That beautiful teacher drove down the alley by St. Mary's Church each morning, and she even thought to tell me not to mention it to the other kids, so they wouldn't call me *teacher's pet*. There's a good chance it was against the rules of the

16. Mrs. Schleser's 4th Grade. These youngsters would be part of my life right up to graduation from TCHS. Photo courtesy of John Dunn.

Front Row: Melba Bradshaw, me, Janice Biery, Renee Larrey, Mary Nell Hunt, Penny Speed, Armelia Nelson, Mary McCoy.

Second row: ?, David Calhoun, Sandra Mensch, ?, Raymond McNeel, Jim West, Betty Van Cleave.

Third Row: John Dunn, Donna Saunders, Barbara Blum, ?, Larry LaFont, Ronnie Wilson, Dennis Thompson, Mrs. Schleser.

Back Row: Robert Waggoner, Lanis Elliot, ?, Alonzo Horn, James Coyle.

school district, too, but what was important to her was the welfare of one little girl.

So between the kindness of the Morris family and Mrs. Schleser's efforts on my behalf, it's no wonder I believe to this day Ronnie walked home from the spring carnival with a real live pony in tow. And if you told me the pony spoke to him in French, I'd believe that, too.

Marvels like that happened all the time in Texas City.

CHAPTER THREE

The Butterfly and the Bombardier

April is the cruellest month, breeding
Lilacs out of the dead land, mixing
Memory and desire, stirring
Dull roots with spring rain.

T. S. Eliot, The Waste Land, 1922

No child ever made a more spectacular first impression than I did. My presentation to my extended family late 1946 was so remarkable no one ever forgot it. I only learned the story in April of 2012. April, when Texas is covered in bluebonnets, and my cousin Beverly and I spent a week touring the landscape of our youth.

I live in northern Virginia; she lives in Fort Worth, but after a good deal of planning, I flew to Fort Worth and she picked me up at the airport. We headed south to visit her daughter in Spring, Texas. My scary cousin Ray and his gracious wife Susan hosted a reunion in Dickenson with the remaining offspring of the Sisters Benskin, and the next day Bev and I drove to Texas City.

We spent two euphoric days driving around TC, eating at the Terraza Mexican Bar and Grill, formerly known as the Terrace Drive-in. We took pictures of places we lived and schools we attended, and we met the man who now lives in the Fourth Avenue garage apartment across the alley from St. Mary's Catholic Church, where Bev was once a bride.

17. Bev and me, TC Dike, 2012.

Then we headed into the heart of Texas, to San Saba, Cherokee, and Llano, where our grandparents came from and moved back to when they left Texas City. We visited the graves of our grandparents and great grandparents, and not only did we see the home where our grandparents lived when we were children, we were spotted by the present owner, and she invited us in to look around.

When we were girls, San Saba and Cherokee were small but thriving. Now they're all but shut down, the occasional open café outnumbered by boarded up businesses that used to be. Bev and I, strangers in a sleek white Lexus, stood out. Every time we stopped, someone approached us. If no one was around, someone circled in their truck, got out, and came over.

Can I help you? Looking for someone? Lost, are you?

Toward the end of the trip we pulled up in front of a clapboard house in Cherokee. I didn't remember it, but Bev said our grandparents once lived there, before the house in San Saba. It had a new addition, or a new porch, or maybe a shed had been torn down, but she was sure it was the place.

Her face lit up, the light of remembrance. "There! That's where I saw you for the first time. Right over there."

I don't know if she remembers this tale, or if she heard it so many times she thinks she remembers it - she could only have been three or four years old, but this is the story she told me:

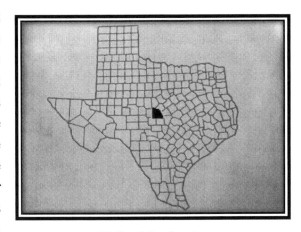

18. San Saba County

"Aunt Hazel (my mother) had been living in Florida, and everyone was so excited she was coming home and bringing her new husband. Then about a week before we were to meet at Grandma's and Papaw's – this house – we got a birth announcement. About you. She hadn't been married long, but she had a husband now and counting it up wasn't important. Everybody just wanted to welcome her home. She was always the life of the party, you know, your mother. So much fun."

I thought I knew all the troubling details of my birth. However, Beverly's excitement in relating the tale made me sense there would be something new here.

"Yup." She continued. "We drove up, and your mother was sitting on the porch, and there you were. One month old. You jumped off the step and started gathering up pecans. You had a ball, and there was a dog, I think. When you saw the car, you waved! My parents just stared. I didn't understand, of course, and then my dad said, "Either that's the most amazing baby in history, or that kid's at least a year old!"

The part of the story that got to me was not what I already knew. What made me laugh out loud was how exactly like my mother that overdue birth announcement was.

She had married, but she had been away, and no one knew she had a child who pre-dated the wedding. She was longing for Texas, so she was cornered. I can hear her thoughts: *Oh, dear. What now? I'm going home, and everyone will be shocked. They don't know I have a baby. Hmmm. I know. I'll send out birth announcements! I'll just leave off the year.*

19. Cherokee. Something beautiful about it, but sad.

And that's what she did. She didn't think no one would notice, but it seemed a great way to lessen the surprise. A perfect solution! And that Benskin reunion goes down in family lore as The Reunion We Met Becky, the running, jumping, ball-throwing, 25-pound newborn infant.

And this brings me to the story of the Butterfly and the Bombardier, and it's a hard story to tell, or even to decide to tell. My mother was ashamed of what happened in Florida, and I wish I could ask her if I can tell it now. But every family – no exceptions – has a story like this. She told me most of it herself; only the birth announcement was new. Did she think I might share it someday? She knew I was a writer. One thing for sure, she had a flair for drama, and she knew it was a good story.

All the players are gone from this earth, my grandparents, my parents, my aunts and uncles. Only a few people are alive who remember my mother, so the story can only matter now in the human and universal sense. I considered leaving out one or two crucial details, but then it wouldn't be the truth, and understanding her story is to understand something about a

20. Bev standing near the spot where we first met.

whole generation of women. There's something in it of mothers and daughters, too.

So here's the story of the Butterfly and the Bombardier. They never should have met, and if it wouldn't cancel out my own existence, I would wish they never had.

For 30 years I thought my father was my mother's first husband, but in the course of time I learned he wasn't. The reason her once-happy home in Texas City had become intolerable is another story, but because it had, when she was still a teenager, she saw marriage to an older man as a way out. There weren't many options for women at the time. Stay home like a good girl, work in a dime store, or get married. A few women went to college and had careers, but not many in Texas in the '40s.

21. Jinx with an admirer, early in the war. This photo captures the spirit of the times.

The war had started, and my mother's first husband, Ervin, was in the Navy, so when he was sent to San Diego for training, she went with him. Their marriage was unusual from the start. For instance, in deference to her young age and unsown wild oats, he allowed her to date. Yes, she told me that. Her dates picked her up on the front porch of their rented house and dropped her there when the evening was over. Her husband didn't mind as long as she didn't stay out too late. This still floors me.

When Ervin shipped out to the Pacific, my mother went home to Texas. Her older sister Jackie was married, and her younger sister Jinx had just graduated from high school. Jinx and my mother were like a powder keg and a spark. They dared each other to laugh louder, dance longer.

They had cousins living in Florida, and it seemed like a good idea to go somewhere. They headed to Tampa, moved in with the cousins, and had the time of their lives. There was a war on, there were military bases in the area, the place was crawling with handsome young men in uniform and lovely girls who saw the rules as suspended, if not exactly cancelled.

Tomorrow we die was in the air. By this time my mother knew she had married the wrong man for the wrong reasons. She hadn't seen Irvin in over two years. She barely remembered him at all. She was young and full of life.

Enter the Bombardier. Richard Wenrick Bagley.

Someone brought him to the house where she lived. When he saw my mother for the first time, he said: "Jesus. Look at the head on that one."

She was sitting in the middle of the living room floor winding her hair into pin curls. As a pick-up line, I guess it worked, because they became an item. They were both 23 years old. He was still in the Army, but his war was over due to injuries sustained in Germany.

22. The Bombardier, 1952.

What do I know about my father? Not much. My mother didn't talk about him. I once asked my Aunt Jinx, who knew him, to tell me something good about him. I knew the bad stuff – I saw it with my own eyes.

Aunt Jinx thought for a minute. "Well," she said. "He liked the ladies, and the ladies liked him. He was funny and fun. If he was in the crowd, we knew we would have a good time." She shrugged. That's all she could offer.

I remember my father's paintings, which I've been told are displayed in galleries in upstate New York. I remember a painting of a hen and her chicks, so vividly wrought I wanted to cuddle a chick and stroke its fuzzy pale head. His art was going to make us rich.

23. The Butterfly about the time of her first marriage (from an old locket).

He invented things, tools and toys, one in particular, a small boat he crafted from light-weight wood. He put a balloon inside and fixed the nozzle end so the air would empty into the water. When the air came out, the little boat moved across the bathtub leaving a bubbly, cheerful wake. He named it "JeTTug," with the middle Ts in caps. The toy was going to make us rich.

I also remember him coming home drunk and beating up my mother, and that's the last time I'll mention this, except to say that when I was six years old I promised myself no one would ever, ever treat me that way, and no one ever has.

I don't know the nature of my father's war injury, at least not the one that showed. My father's mother told me that before the war he never drank, and the worst he did was steal his sister's dolls and put them up in trees. She said he was a born artist, gone to the Army, taught to sit in the nose of a B-24 and drop the bombs.

He must have been cold and terrified, and back home he had nightmares of killing little babies and old people in cities he would never visit. My grandmother said it ruined him, and it wasn't supposed to. Both the efficacy and the morality of the carpet bombings in World War II have been re-examined, but at the time he was supposed to feel righteous and get on with his happy life.

Instead, before the war ended, before he mustered out, before they were married, he turned to drink and the consoling arms of my mother.

Line breaks in poetry don't occur by accident. Like turning points in our lives, the breaks in Eliot's poem emphasize, underscore, and create a theme. Breeding – mixing – stirring – roots – rain.

**24. The only example I have of my father's art,
a pencil drawing done when he was a boy.**

In Texas in April all the breeding, mixing, stirring and rain breeds bluebonnets, not lilacs. My mother in hot, wet Florida. My father just back from the war with a purple heart that didn't help his broken heart. In Florida in April the mixing and stirring between the Butterfly and the Bombardier resulted in me, accidentally and inconveniently. An understatement.

They were in love, but in point of fact, and no matter how young she was, she was married to someone else, someone away fighting for his country, when she became pregnant with me. And no matter what the war did to him, a man isn't supposed to abuse a woman.

My mother divorced Ervin and married my father within a week, and her family knew of the divorce and remarriage. But she was so ashamed no one knew about me for over a year. Back then if a woman was *in trouble*, it meant one thing. As the family historian, I'm in possession of a lot of old letters, some from my mother to my grandmother, and because of the dates, I know I existed, but there's nothing about dashing off a word while the baby's sleeping. Nothing about a runny nose, a new toy, or cooing or hair or smiles for the first time. Nothing.

25. My mother and me. Neither of us look too happy.

I doubt my mother even remembered the fanciful, way-late birth announcement.

This final piece of the puzzle slipped into place for me in April of 2012, 67 years after the fact. Because Bev and I, cousins and friends, decided to take a road trip into the past, I learned about my debut in the front yard of that little house in Cherokee, where I made the kind of impression relatives talked about for years.

Knowing my mother, and how she liked to be the center of attention, how she liked a good story, and loved her family, and loved a good laugh, I think she would approve of this telling.

Because of the events in this story, I grew up sensing an ambivalence in my mother's attitude toward me. Being a mother myself, I know that no matter how happy the event, mixed feelings are born with every first child. Your own girlhood is over, whether you're 14 or 40. Nothing will ever be the same, not when they're out of diapers, not when they graduate from high school. Not the same, not ever. What I knew about my parents forced me to wonder if I was the worst thing that ever happened to my mother.

This last is not a hazy memory, or a second-hand account. This is what happened when my mother died, in the very room where I would one day write her story.

If all things aren't healed by time, time does allow for closure and peace. As she lay dying the Butterfly squeezed my hand and answered a question she knew I would never ask. The last thing she said before she slipped into a deep sleep and then slipped away, was this: "You're the best thing that ever happened to me."

26. My mother the Butterfly in 2005, nine months
before her death. She had just voted for the first time.

CHAPTER FOUR

Danise and the Magic Summers

What lasts?

Friendships, summers, memories, and the mashed potato spoon, large and sturdy, perfect for scooping globs of buttery mashed potatoes onto your plate, back when carbs didn't matter. That spoon is the only thing I have that also lived in the Fourth Avenue garage apartment, and I treasure it. In case of fire, my house could be ablaze, and I'd be standing in the street clutching the mashed potato spoon.

27. Danise (left) and me, Galveston, late '50s

Memories last, and as for summers, I never revisit the last summers of my childhood without thinking of Danise Louise Miller.

Here's the first thing she said when she came to me, almost 60 years ago: "You're a girl."

Good luck can turn on something as simple as one little girl speaking to another.

I was outside on the open wooden steps to our apartment. The neighboring garage was about 10 feet away, so the steps leading up to our apartment over the garage were in a canyon. It was a private place, and I liked it. I still attended fourth grade across town, but I knew there were other kids around. I saw them from a window, but I was not capable of seeking them out.

I wondered, if I could transform myself into a merry-go-round, would the other kids come to me? Even as I had the thought, a brown flighty thing flashed by, visible for a moment in the opening between the two garages. I took it for a bird until I heard a stopping sound in the oyster shell alley, and it came back. It was a little girl all of one color, tan skin, tan hair, tan eyes, skinny and small, and a little dirty. When kids played outside all day, they got dirty. By summer's end outdoor children, after the evening bath, glowed from sunshine, fresh air, exercise, and freedom.

The bird creature stared at me, and I stared back. It's a suspended moment, just as it is, forever in my mind, and it only moves forward when she speaks again, repeats her opening line: "You're a girl."

The message that being male was better than being female had sneaked into my head, inculcated. That's a good word, inculcated. Male bias was in the culture. I didn't know whether her remark was a statement or an accusation. She stepped closer. "There's only boys on the block, except for me. My baby sisters don't count. I'm Danise. I live three houses down."

I didn't like the part about the boys. Although Mrs. Schleser's fourth grade almost cured my fear of boys, my experience before that was bad. I started first grade in a country school outside San Antonio, and I walked home alone through a woods. Freddy ambushed me often, pulled my braids, called me a girl, and threw my books to the ground. He did little more than scare me, but I reported it to my mother, who shrugged and said it meant he liked me.

By second grade I attended a different country school, and Junior Jim (he was called that) sought me out and punched me in the stomach for fun, and that hurt. When I told

28. John Dunn, one of Mrs. Schleiser's fourth grade gentlemen.

the teacher, she called me a tattle tale. It only meant he liked me, she said. When I got a belly full of Junior Jim liking me, I picked up a hefty piece of fallen mesquite wood, planted my feet, and warned him. Hesitation. He wasn't convinced I would hit him, but he wasn't convinced I wouldn't, either. I didn't know for sure myself, but something rose in me, hard and ready, and I thought I might. He left me alone after that, and I became a believer in the "show of force" defense. I was seven, and not strong, but win or lose, I could at least look like I would fight back.

In Mrs. Schleser's class the boys behaved like gentlemen, Dennis Thompson, John Dunn, Raymond McNeel, all of them. They talked too much and spilled things, but they didn't hurt anyone. Such behavior wouldn't have been tolerated by teachers, parents, the principal, the janitor, or even an adult passer-by. Still, I had my reservations about boys. I ruminated on the boy problem, but finally I caught on. I was supposed to say something to the little girl, Danise.

"Oh. I'm Becky. I'm 10. I live right here."

"Do you wanna play with me?" She smiled her gentle smile.

Do you wanna play with me? Was it a trick question? Maybe not. My cousin Bev seemed to like me. Renee had invited me to her house. Danise sensed I would require a little time.

At last, I said, "Yes. Thank you. I would like to play with you." Such a formal acceptance. I probably curtsied, but I didn't smile, I'm sure. I was too busy thinking things to death.

29. My mother, about 1956.

"Come on then. I'll show you the neighborhood!"

It must have been a weekend morning, because my mother was home. She worked weekdays, and Friday and Saturday nights she went out. Sunday nights, too. I ran up the stairs, told her there was a little girl, and we were going to walk around. I scrambled back down.

We started up the alley exchanging information. She went to Danforth Elementary school, and I explained I would be attending Danforth next fall. We would both be in fifth grade. Perhaps we would have the same teacher! She pointed out the sites, like the chinaberry trees and the outdoor faucet where you could always get a drink of water. She explained in a whisper that sometimes you could see priests walking around at the catholic church just across the ally, all in black-and-white, like penguins. Then she brightened.

She told me the Catholic trash barrels were filled by the priests every day with perfectly good envelopes and paper, sometimes candles. The wet garbage was elsewhere, so the barrels were fun to rummage through.

30. Beautiful mission-style St. Mary's Catholic Church.

Later on, we would dare each other to sneak into St. Mary's and risk the wrath of the Catholic God, who everyone knew was fiercer than the Protestant God. The church was dim after the bright sun, and quiet, so quiet. One time we tiptoed all the way to the altar and picked up something that had brass bells on it. The ringing exploded in the silence and sent two bad little girls scrambling like the Holy Ghost was on our tail! Out the front door, over the grass, and across the alley to collapse in a pile of giggles behind the garage apartment, safe! No lightning bolts from above, nor penguin priests giving chase!

But that was yet to come, and as we left the church behind, she pointed to a vacant lot. "That's where we play softball. I'm a tomboy. I like to run and climb trees."

It sounded like fun. Dolls bored me, but I didn't mention it; it seemed wrong. I was a girl. I was supposed to love dolls, and I was eager to be like my new friend. "I'm a tomboy, too."

She showed me Bobby's house, a duplex connected by a garage to Andrew's house. We turned and walked down 13th Street toward Fourth Avenue.

"Over there, that's Darrell's house. Kenny lives down there - he's different." She said this as she would have said Kenny has blue eyes. It was only a statement, and I took it for what it was: information.

She shared her personal dossier on the Fourth Avenue boys: Bobby, cute but only a rising fourth grader. Andrew, pretty dull. Darrell, nice, serious. Kenny, of course. It took him a long time to finish high school, and then he went into the Army.

One time Kenny came over, and the other kids tried to shoo him away. Danise wouldn't have it. She said everyone could play. Kenny, too. And that was that. He was big, and we made him be the creature from the black lagoon or the invader from outer space, not from meanness, but because he could pick one of us up and carry us

31. Serious Darrell Barger from Fourth Avenue, first scout on the Left. From *Images of America - Texas City*, by Albert L. Mitchell.

32. Back row, Johnny Murphy, Kenny Gentry, and Harold ?. Front, my sister Tish, me and Danise, about 1957 or '58, after a dusting of snow.

off as the others gave chase. He never seemed to mind. He was glad to be in the gang, and he had Danise to thank for it.

The tour proceeded down Fourth Avenue, and with a sigh, she pointed to a house on the left. "Johnny lives there. He's in sixth grade. That's his bike. When it's there, I know he's home."

I could tell she was in love with him, so I decided to fall in love with him, too. Although she saw him first, she didn't mind sharing, and our "older man" came and went quickly, breaking neither of our hearts in any significant way. He was cute, though.

We stopped in front of a clapboard rental house in need of

33. Bobby Burgin in 10th grade. He looked the same in 3rd grade.

34. Danise and her mother, October 2006.

paint. "I live here." She walked onto the porch and disappeared inside, but I held back. "Well, come on," she said. "I'll show you to my mother. My dad's at work."

I loved this new thing, *Dad at Work.* Uncle Raymond went to work. Danise's dad went to work. The whole time I lived in Texas City, I never met anyone whose Dad didn't go to work.

We went to the back of the house, where a pretty lady stood by the kitchen sink, up to her elbows in a bowl of dough. Danise's mother seemed old because I was 10, and because my own glamorous single mother worked hard at not seeming old.

Mrs. Miller slipped a towel from her shoulder and wiped her hands. "Who's this?"

"It's Becky. She's a girl."

Mrs. Miller smiled, the same sweet smile she had passed on to Danise. "Well, I can see that. Where'd you get her?"

"She moved into Mrs. Wagoner's garage apartment."

"Good! And you're in time to spoon-drop these cookies. I'll bet you like cookies, don't you, Becky?"

I certainly did - snickerdoodles, they were - and from then on Mrs. Miller took me everywhere with her brood, and she taught me to bake cookies and hem skirts. She was kind and intuitive, too. Before the first batch of cookies came out of the oven, she knew way more about me than I told her. She knew I missed my parents. I didn't want to talk about my father, and my mother was busy being a divorcée, though she called herself a widow (her charming way of dealing with unpleasantness).

Whether deliberately or by default, Mrs. Miller began to fill in for the Butterfly. Danise made sure I was integrated into the neighborhood, and so began a summer that lasted three years. We went to school, and perhaps it got cold, but in my memory from fourth grade through sixth, it's always summer.

I learned too young I would have to look after myself, but I was relieved to have a friend to help sometimes, like when I got into a fist fight with Bobby. He and I often butted heads, and after one colorful exchange of insults, he got riled up and slapped me in the face. He didn't think of this as hitting a girl - I was just Becky from the block.

In one instant the world went scarlet. I threw myself at him full throttle, and we tumbled to the ground, thrashing away. Danise realized that in 10 seconds I would lose the element of surprise, and Bobby was going to kick the living crap out of me. He was strong, and I was no match for him. Danise added herself to the twisted pile of arms and legs, and in the three-way scuffle she managed to pull us apart. When we were all upright again, she stood between Bobby and me until our tempers passed, and we all went home.

We played games of imagination and fun, influenced by movies and comic books. Our favorites were Roy Rogers and Dale Evans (Bobby loved to be Roy) and Robin Hood, and although Danise or I insisted on being Robin now and then, we couldn't prevail on Bobby to be Maid Marian.

We could walk on hot coals by July, the soles of our bare feet got so thick, and we wore pink or yellow sunsuits, tied at the shoulders, available for three dollars at Penny's down on Sixth Street. We played hide-and-seek in the dusk and after dark put lightning bugs

35. The TC swimming pool in 2006. It looked the same for many
years. The high school stadium can be seen in the background.

in glass jars. There were pomegranates to smash on the street and
watch from windows as fierce afternoon storms washed the seeds
away.

Danise and I hid in dark, cool places where our sisters
couldn't find us. We climbed chinaberry trees for ammunition, and
had epic chinaberry fights. When we had a quarter for a ticket and a
nickel for candy, we walked to the Showboat down on Sixth Street.
Sometimes we stopped at the Ben Franklin store for ten cents worth of
warm cashews to share. Stale as they were, we were sure they made us
very, very cool.

We loved the attic of the old library on Ninth Avenue, where
the dripping window air-conditioner kept us cool and provided white
noise, and we were astonished to learn we could check out as many
books as we wanted, in a place and time when there were limits to
everything.

We spent so many hours at the public swimming pool
Danise's ash blond hair took on a greenish tinge. We went every other

**36. Kids hanging out in the attic of the old library. From
Images of America - Texas City, by Albert L. Mitchell.**

day, even though we had to bike Gobi-like distances. We rode "no-hands" and pretended to splash through water mirages, and our legs grew strong as our little sisters trailed behind.

We took free dance classes at the recreation center where Mrs. Kehoe, the local dance teacher, donated her time. We crushed on Robert, her assistant, the only boy who came near the dancing classes.

We took our sandals to King's Shoe Shop down on Sixth Street to have taps put on the toes, and we met Gene King, the handsome red-headed son of the owner. Just our age, he charmed us both as he did the work. On the way home, we stopped at the post office,

37. Robert Huffman

just to roll on the grassy man-made hill, all of a two-foot slant.

By the time we got back to Fourth Avenue, it would be afternoon, and how pleasant it was before every 10-foot square bit of lawn required an insane number of power machines. There was the gentle sound of a revolving mower and the scrape of a rake mixed with birdsong and the laughter of children. In the evenings mothers called their kids who came reluctantly home, reluctant until they caught the smells from the kitchen and realized they were hungry, so hungry getting home couldn't happen fast enough.

We shared the joy of growing up and feeling safe in a town where no one seemed rich, and no one seemed poor, and even though there wasn't much to be had on my mother's earnings, I didn't care because no one else seemed to. Time spent with the Fourth Avenue gang cured me of my boy-fear, and by the time the halcyon summers ended, boy people were just people.

Remember those little Brownie cameras we held waist-high? We pretended to see the future photo framed in the square on top, but

38. The Sixth Street post office on the "hill." From
Images of America - Texas City, **by Albert L. Mitchell.**

we couldn't. Not really, any more than we could see our own future or predict what would last a lifetime.

Memories, beautiful and intact. The mashed potato spoon is indestructible, and so is my friendship with Danise. Yes, we experienced a long period of separation, like sisters who realize they have to go their own way to find out who they really are, beyond the influence of each other. Time brought us together again.

39. Danise through a Brownie camera (see cover photo), stylishly *Grease* ahead of her time.

Danise and the Magic Summers. Sounds like a children's book, to be read at bedtime and dreamed of in the deep sleep of childhood.

To be dreamed of, because that's what didn't last. By the time we had children of our own, the endless green summers had vanished, and forever, like the ice cream truck that played *Twinkle Twinkle Little Star* as mothers called their children home.

CHAPTER FIVE

The Bruskins

"Ah, the Bruskins. See you on Sunday, Sweetie."

Aunt Venita flicked her gold-bangled wrist, rolled up the car window and sped away.

40. Aunt Venita Benskin with my sister Tish, 1956.

I was walking home from Danise's house when my aunt happened to drive by, in a hurry as always, but it would have been rude not to stop. I wished I could see the stylish high-heeled shoes she usually wore to show off her fabulous legs. In a few years we would wear the same shoe size, and if they pinched her toes, she would pass the shoes on to me. I loved them because they once belonged to her. I still like to sit in my sun room in the morning, wearing a robe that belonged to my mother. It's more than the sun making me feel warm.

Her Bruskin remark was in response to my bit of small talk, which was about my grandparents coming for Easter. *See you on Sunday* meant she would be at Aunt Jackie's for Easter dinner with the whole family.

Easter was a big deal, beyond the religious significance. In April the weather is pleasant in Texas for up to 30 minutes at a time, and the bluebonnets are out, which makes everyone joyful. I feel sorry for anyone who hasn't looked upon the glory of rolling Texas hills turned blue as far as you can see. It is a singular pleasure.

41. Venita Benskin, 98 years old.

Bruskins? My grandparents were the *Benskins*. Did I hear wrong?

Aunt Venita's attention was elsewhere even before she drove away. I loved the lady, but if you got one thought in before she started talking again, you were lucky. I saw her for the last time in

2012. She was 98 years old, and she listened long enough to figure out who I was, then she filled me in on everything she ate, drank, and wore since the last time we met over 30 years before.

I took her picture and showed her the preview. "Look how pretty you are."

"Oh, sweet Jesus. I look like hell." Ninety-eight years old, and that's what she said.

But back to Fourth Avenue. I was 11 or 12, and the neighborhood kids were crawling all over outside as usual. Johnny came by on his bike, and circled me twice, a la *The Wild One*. Theaters in town avoided showing movies that might be a "bad influence on our youth," so he probably never saw it, but everyone knew about *The Wild One*. Marlon Brando was even called "Johnny." Fourth Avenue Johnny was in 7th grade at Blocker Junior High, and in a bad-boy phase, white t-shirt, hair slicked back in a greasy duck tail. The playing card on his bicycle spokes didn't really sound like a motorcycle, but I didn't mention it.

He demanded to know why Mrs. Benskin stopped to speak to me. He knew her from school, he said.

I shrugged. "She's my aunt."

He looked dumbfounded. "Mrs. Benskin is your AUNT? Boy, do you have it MADE!"

Aunt Venita was the secretary at Blocker for years. I didn't see how this was going to help me, but it did once, during final exams in ninth grade. I made it back from lunch seconds after the bell rang, and tardiness was not tolerated. The vice principal, Mr. Sowers, loomed like a skinny bat, waiting to banish us all. No hall passes. No final exam. Go home. This was a calamity. From her office Aunt Venita spotted me looking like hara-kiri would be my next test.

What would happen to me now? I would fail English. I would not graduate from junior high, and thus not from high school. My mother would kill me dead. My reputation would be ruined. Aunt Jackie would hate me. One last full-bore junior high catastrophe.

Aunt Venita motioned me into her office and asked what class I had next. She scribbled a note and handed it to me. *Mrs. Schaeffer, Please excuse Becky for being tardy. She was helping me in the office. Mrs. Benskin.*

She had a steely gaze when she could focus long enough, and she warned me she would never do this again. My family didn't make empty threats or empty promises. If they said it, they meant it, but I'd been taken off death row, and I didn't care about the other late-comers who didn't have Aunt Venita to save them. Let them die.

She had things to do, so she stood up and walked away in her high heels, and I scurried off to class, worshipping my aunt and so full of adrenalin I aced my English final. When I think of my days at Blocker, I hear the staccato click-click-click of her heels down that marble hall, and when I hear the word savior, I'm supposed to think of Jesus, but I think of Aunt Venita.

**42. Me and my braids.
I did not love them.**

After Johnny foretold the usefulness of having my aunt at Blocker, I could see his attention dribbling away, so I put one hand on my hip and whipped my braids around, nearly putting my own eye out. I didn't have that move down right, apparently, and he rode off, impervious to my elementary school attempt at flirtation. I went home and asked my mother about the Bruskins.

"Where did you hear that? Oh. Venita. Well, it's nothing you need to know about. Or mention. I don't remember. Something a long time ago between your grandma and Papaw's sisters. Della or Louella, if I know those two. Maybe Leola. There were a lot of 'em, and they ganged up on your grandma sometimes. There were hurt feelings."

My mother was a terrible liar and avoided lying unless she had to, so I could tell she really didn't remember. And what she said made sense. My grandmother could bear a grudge for a hundred years, and there were occasional family dust-ups between the women, usually during the holidays. The men stayed in the garage, willing to shuck bushel baskets full of oysters if they could be left alone to drink beer, tell lies, and talk about Kitirik. Such an innocent time. It never occur to anyone a shapely girl in a cat suit might be wrong for a kid's TV show.

I made it my mission to find out about the Bruskins, because I was obsessed with all things family. I had lost not only my father, but cousins I loved, aunts, too, and my Babo, my father's mother. I adored her. The divorce left me with a fear of losing my mother's family, too.

Aunt Venita was married to my Uncle Grover, who was my grandfather's brother, so he was my great uncle. My mother grew up calling him uncle, but Venita couldn't stand to be called *aunt* by grown-up

43. Kitirik

women, so my mother called her by her given name only. Venita's boys, on the other hand, called my mother *Aunt* Hazel, though she was their first cousin. She was another generation, so it would have been disrespectful to call her Hazel. I loved all this. As for the Bruskins, just because my mother didn't remember where it came from didn't mean I couldn't find out. On Easter Sunday I might get a chance to ask, and I would certainly get to see what Aunt Venita was wearing. She always dressed elegantly. She would see what I was wearing, too, especially my hat.

Easter sent the ladies into a hat-buying frenzy, even though no one under the age of 50 went near a hat the other 364 days a year. At Easter even the Catholic ladies swapped their head doilies for hats. Mine, a thing that might double as a Frisbee, was wrapped in tissue awaiting its 12-hour life span.

Also permissible were bonnets with huge brims. Hats with sexy veils were not allowed. It was EASTER, not Mardi Gras, Aunt Venita once remarked, like she forgot her own hat flaunted a fetching little veil.

In fact, when I wander through my family photos, only three

44. Grandma Benskin and Jackie Benskin by the car, 1920s.

occasions exist. Easter (hats and/or bluebonnets), Christmas (dolls and/or ornament corsages), and permutations of go-stand-by-the-car, where all other photos were taken. Go stand by the car in your bathing suit. Go stand by the car with the deer on the hood. Go stand by the car because we're leaving or arriving. Go stand by the car because we love the car.

So Easter came, the hats were on, and we assembled in Aunt Jackie's pretty living room awaiting the wonderful food, all made by her hand, except for desserts, which were brought by others, but also made by hand.

I saw my chance. There was room on the couch beside Aunt Venita. My grandma was on the other side of the room.

I made sure I had Aunt Venita's attention. "Do you like my hat?"

"Yes, Sweetie. Very nice."

I'd have to be quick or she would mentally be elsewhere. "What's the Bruskins?"

"Where did you hear that old nugget?" she asked.

I thought my brain would explode. Did she really say that about the thing she said to me in the first place?

"What!?" This from my grandmother across the room. The feather on her hat quivered.

Uh oh. My grandmother had this *tone*. When you heard it, something bad was about to happen to someone. I hoped it wouldn't be me, but it was. Aunt Venita grabbed my face and compressed my cheeks between her fingers until I thought my teeth would pop out.

"She said she's bruised her chin." Aunt Venita turned my face from side to side. "I don't see anything, Sweetie."

45. Grandma Benskin, Easter in Aunt Jackie's living room.

My grandma's eyes narrowed, and her mouth was an evil little rosette that began to open. Something horrible would come out. Everyone knew it. My sister Tish was only seven years old, but her round black eyes told me even she knew it.

The miracle that Easter was Aunt Jackie's superb timing. She sensed trouble. Food trumped everything, so she stood up and announced dinner, even though the table wasn't set. My mother and Aunt Venita jumped up with her. Dishes clattered and hats were removed. I was saved. The Bruskins could wait, but I had learned for sure it was about my grandma.

46. Easter. If we weren't by the car, we were in Aunt Jackie's living room. She hosted all holidays for 10 years and more.

When we got home, I chose my moment. My mother spent 90 minutes every day of her life on her make-up, an hour to apply it and 30 minutes to remove it. This was prime time to garner her attention as she sat still at her make-up table.

"I asked Aunt Venita about the Bruskins. Grandma got upset."

The Butterfly hovered with a tissue full of cold cream midway to her face. "I knew she was about to be upset about something. I told you not to mention that."

She went back to removing her Easter makeup. That was all I would get, but I was determined to find out more. By the family picnic on Memorial Day, I had been plotting for weeks, and I singled out my cousin Jim, one of Aunt Venita's sons. Because they were older, I didn't see much of him or his brother Don, but Jim was closest to my age, and he seemed incapable of rational thought. (I was wrong about that. He eventually earned a PhD.) Maybe he would blurt out the truth about the Bruskins without thinking it through first.

I sat down beside him at the picnic. "So, Jim. Howya doin'?"

He was focused on a plate of fried chicken and baked beans, so he didn't look up. I guess he thought his own sneakers had spoken to him.

"Fine." A bean dropped from his mouth.

"What's the Bruskins?"

"I dunno. Uncle Charley and Aunt Ruby? She's crazy, you know." Back to his chicken.

His Aunt Ruby and Uncle Charley were my grandparents. So my grandparents were the *Bruskins*. I had that figured out, but what did it mean? But now I had something else to think about. My grandma was crazy?

47. Papaw Benskin and his brother Grover, with baby in boots and deer on the hood, by the car.

48. Cousin Jim Benskin

There were little things. She sang off-key, loudly, at the merciless Church of Christ summer tent revivals which she made me attend whenever I happened to be in San Saba in August. She scotch-taped strange pictures to the walls in her house, like a newspaper photo of Siamese twins playing the saxophone. My Aunt Jackie's name wasn't Jacqueline, as most people assumed, but *Jack. Jack Armeta.* My grandparents wanted a boy, picked out the name, and when the baby was a girl, called her Jack anyway. My grandmother nagged my grandfather mercilessly, but I thought that might stop if he took the trash out the first time he was asked instead of the sixth or seventh. She seemed odd, maybe, but not crazy.

I couldn't wait to ask my mother, though I didn't bring up the Bruskins. Twice I was told not to talk about it. As usual, the question came directly out of my mouth, by-passing tact altogether.

"Is Grandma crazy?"

She stopped removing her picnic makeup. "Who said that? Jim Benskin? He's just like Venita. He speaks more than he thinks."

"So Grandma isn't crazy?" I can still hear the sigh of the Butterfly as she considered her answer.

"OK, some people say she is. When she gets wound up, she can seem pretty crazy. There's a crazy

49. Cousin Don Benskin

gene or something that gets worse if bad things happen to you, and God knows she has reason to be really crazy. Crazy like insane. But she isn't insane. She's just a little crazy. Every crazy family is crazy in its own way."

I doubt if my mother ever heard the famous lines from Tolstoy, *All happy families are alike; each unhappy family is unhappy in its own way*, but I had just been doomed to hear that quote differently for the rest of my life. *Each crazy family is crazy in its own way.*

I see the Benskin craziness now. It's a kind of paranoia, nothing major, just the sense that any one of us could turn weird any moment, misinterpret something, misunderstand and pounce. Saying the wrong thing is my specialty, but at least I've learned it's best to say nothing most of the time.

And all families are crazy. When I talk about my family, and tell some of the craziness, without exception, I hear this:

"You think your family's crazy? Wait 'til you hear about my family."

And the race is on: my-family-is-crazier-than-your-family. All families are zany, weirdly, fabulously, humanly nuts. I have known a couple of exceptions; I've lived long enough to find exceptions to everything, but over all? Yup. Crazy.

And here's something. The exceptions are boring as pudding. They don't laugh too loud, or get angry, or belch in public. They don't call each other names or miss church. Their slips never show; their hair never moves. They make sensible decisions and never re-gift. No swimming after eating, no silly trips overseas. No slap and tickle, and no hats with veils, especially on Easter. That's pretty emphatically not the Benskins.

I finally lost interest in the Bruskin business. It was a dead-end, and probably nothing much anyway. However, when the age of the internet arrived, I was able to find out family things I never imagined. While browsing around Ancestry.com, I came across something. It took 50 years, but there they were. The Bruskins.

It was only a minor mystery after all, and I failed to see what

50. My mother by the longest car ever made. I think it was a 1959 Pontiac. I actually drove this beast.

all the fuss was about. I printed the page. My mother read it, and although my grandma died in 1973, she was fully resurrected in that moment.

"I remember now," my mother said. "Your grandma went to the county clerk or something. See here?" She pointed to her own name on the list. "I was only nine. She raised a stink that went on for weeks, and Papaw's sisters thought she was crazy to care. They started calling her *Ruby the Bruskin,* and she got her feelings hurt. She stayed mad about it for years."

ancestry.com

1930 United States Federal Census

Name:	**Charles W Bruskin**
Home in 1930:	Texas City, Galveston, Texas
Age:	35
Estimated birth year:	abt 1895
Birthplace:	Texas
Relation to Head of House:	Head
Spouse's name:	Ruby E
Race:	White

Household Members: Name	Age
Charles W Bruskin	35
Ruby E Bruskin	34
Jack A Bruskin	12
Hazel A Bruskin	9
Dorothy F Bruskin	6

51. The misspelling of *Benskin* on the 1930 census.

My mother was full of nonsense, most of it misspelled. To her, any word worth writting down deserrved a set of doubble letters. Still, she could do math in her head faster than anyone I ever knew, and her flighty charm was punctuated with flashes of insight. She made observations about people now and then that hit the mark so square she should have been a sniper.

"Your grandmother grew up very poor, and motherless, too, way out in San Saba County. She felt like trash, and she hated it when she and her sisters got church charity and old clothes. It made her feel like she was nobody, and never would be anybody."

She handed the paper back to me. "Then for a while in Texas City, she was somebody. Papaw owned a business, and she was in the proper ladies' clubs. I don't know the details, but she tried to fix this." She teared up, and I waited while she regained her composure. "She was proud to be Mrs. Charley Benskin, and she felt like she counted. She wanted to count."

The length and breadth of my grandparents' story bears telling, but I'll save it for another time. What I found on Ancestry was silly and funny to me, but because of what my mother told me I realized why it hurt my grandmother in a way her sisters-in-law didn't understand.

52. The *Bruskin* family, so-named forever in the U.S. Census of 1930. My mother is standing next to my grandmother.

The census entry shows how my grandparents and their children were recorded in 1930: Charles, Ruby, Jack, Hazel and Dorothy, Bruskins forever, all of them. It made Ruby *Benskin* feel like a poor country orphan again, like she still didn't count and never would. And nothing she could do would ever change it.

CHAPTER SIX

Reappear the Bombardier

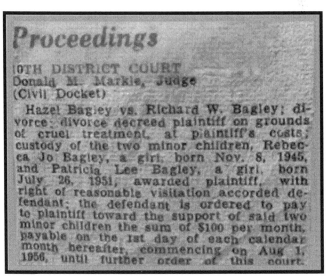

Proceedings

10TH DISTRICT COURT
Donald M. Markle, Judge
(Civil Docket)

Hazel Bagley vs. Richard W. Bagley; divorce: divorce decreed plaintiff on grounds of cruel treatment, at plaintiff's costs; custody of the two minor children, Rebecca Jo Bagley, a girl, born Nov. 8, 1945, and Patricia Lee Bagley, a girl, born July 26, 1951, awarded plaintiff, with right of reasonable visitation accorded defendant; the defendant is ordered to pay to plaintiff toward the support of said two minor children the sum of $100 per month, payable on the 1st day of each calendar month hereafter, commencing on Aug. 1, 1956, until further order of this court.

**53. From the Texas City Sun. I found this
in my mother's things after her death.**

The seasons change even on the Gulf coast of Texas, but the changes are subtle, a gradual dimming of the heat, birds in V-formation going home, a little less shine on the leaves of ligustrum bushes. A year vanished like that, subtle and slow. My parents were divorced, and Pennsylvania was in the past. A year is long to a child. I loved Danforth Elementary School, I loved the immense sky overhead, and my first and best friend Danise was with me every day.

Still, the relative calm didn't make me stop missing my father, though I tried. I missed my mother, too, but the primary gift of time is understanding. I know now how difficult it was to be divorced with children in 1957. She wasn't married, but she had children, so she wasn't single, either, and she was just out of a 12-year ordeal. She was unmarried in a married town and the sole support of two little girls, no option of a well-paying job. It's not surprising she was worried and preoccupied.

54. My mother shortly before her divorce. Worry shows on her face.

My home-life improved beyond measure when we left my father, yet those times lingered in my mind, one episode in particular. I'm not sure where we were living, but I began having crazy, unknowable nightmares. I coped by refusing to sleep, which made me crabby and difficult. My mother wanted to escape her situation long before she managed it, and my nightmares coincided with the ruination of her first attempt. Could I have sensed her fresh despair?

Because she was pregnant again. Years later she confided in me; she had secretly saved enough money, and she was about to buy two bus tickets out when her morning sickness began.

It broke my heart. She never knew the contentment of carrying a child with joy in her heart, and a good, hard-working man to share it. It was another unhappy pregnancy, though not so traumatic as the first, or maybe it was worse, because there was no hope. When she was big pregnant with Tish, we moved on again. My father wrote bad checks all over San Antonio. She couldn't waitress at the Chicken Shack now, so we headed north to his family, a step ahead of the law.

I can spare a little compassion for my father. He had more demons than I can know, and he was desperate, too.

55. My sister Tish and me in 1956. We look worried, too.

There came a time when my mother needed to talk about those days, and I did, too. Our conversations bounced from place to place, just as our physical locations had in the "old days." I told her about the teacher who called me *Mona Lisa*, and asked why I was so sad, but I had no idea what she was talking about. Another teacher called me a Christmas present, because I arrived in December. I talked about a bridge in New Castle, and how I liked to stare down at the rushing water until it felt like the river was standing still, and I was moving. I didn't know anything about relative motion, but I knew I was always moving.

Once we were safe in our tiny garage apartment in Texas City, my mother tried not to say negative things about my father, but she cringed when she heard his name, and it poked something inside me, a pin prick of pain. If I was half him, and she hated him, did she hate half of me? But I suspect her cringing had as much to do with loving him as hating him. So though the worst was over, my emotional state during that first year could be described as vulnerable, perhaps fragile.

It gets hazy now, because he came unannounced and without warning, on a happy day when I was walking home from school. I can't paint this event into a whole picture. I can only construct it from snatches of half-memory flashing on my mental screen like those movie trailers, the ones that show scenes in bright succession, and you never quite know what it adds up to.

Some things I know. It was fifth grade, because my sister was at the babysitter, and not with me, as she would have been when I was in sixth. I was walking home with Danise. We always walked home together, laughing and talking. So it was on this day. Everything was normal. Danise and I jumped from square to square on the sidewalk, chanting *Step on a crack, break your mother's back*. I became aware of a car on the street, but something was off. It was going too slow, trolling. It should have passed us. Why didn't it pass us?

I looked over and locked eyes with the Bombardier.

He was in the driver's seat of a black car. Remembering the moment seems like swimming. There's a thick resistance, even to the memory. Seeing him sent me into emotional shock. How could he be here, driving down Fourth Avenue? This was Texas City, and he didn't belong here. Shock seeks a way out, a way to change what's happening. If we could get across Sixth Street, I thought, he would be gone, because it couldn't be him. Yet it was.

And there was a woman in the car. Unfair, how strong emotions revisit in memory, love, hate, rage. I feel angry when I remember the woman. I overheard the ugliness in those dark nights when my father came home late and drunk. Among my parents' many problems, there was the problem of other women. As my Aunt Jinx described him, "He liked the ladies, and the ladies liked him." It didn't matter that this was probably a brand new other woman.

I almost remember being drawn closer to his dark brown eyes, the same as mine. I almost remember wanting to get in the car. I almost remember Danise holding on to the back of my red plaid school dress, tugging, refusing to let go. She told me years later she remembered the incident, and thinking if she let me get in that car, she would never see me again.

So I stood frozen and mute on the cracked curb. I couldn't speak, couldn't tell her who it was, wasn't sure I knew.

56. *Speck* in first grade.

Did we walk home with him following? I don't know. I wonder to this day how long it took him to find me. How many afternoons did he lurk outside Roosevelt or Kohfeldt, staring intently at the children as they went along home? Or did he come first to Danforth?

The next thing I know for sure, he was walking into the living room of the garage apartment.

He cast a sneering eye at the second-hand furniture. "This is where you live?"

And he brought his girlfriend in with him. Was I conscious of the wrongness of that? He brought his girlfriend uninvited and intruding into the haven my mother had made for us. My mother, the woman whose heart he broke, but not her spirit. It's so long later, and the memory is still upsetting.

He whispered to the other woman, whose face and form is a blank, but I recall his words exactly. "She's intelligent and sensitive."

He said it with pride, as I stood there trembling.

He asked about my sister, who wouldn't be dropped off home from the babysitter until 5:30, and then he hugged me. I wanted to pull away, but he smelled like my father, and this had an effect which I loved and hated. My emotions ran up and down a scale I've seldom experienced.

"Remember Mountaintop, Speck?" he asked. "You swam in the pool every day." He put his hand on my cheek. I see it: He's sitting in a chair, and I'm standing.

Speck. A pet name, a play on *Becky*, given to me when I was small, and he said I was just a little speck when he looked down at me. And Mountaintop. Both names took me to a happy time, when I was old enough to know how things were, but not old enough to know how wrong they were.

He used the memory like ammunition. Mountaintop. I did love it. It was a fantasy place. I loved Mountaintop, and he knew it. Google Mountaintop Nightclub, and there's a column on local history in the San Antonio Express-News.

Question: Do you have any information on the old Hilltop nightclub near Camp Bullis?

Answer: This sounds like the Mountaintop Dinner Club . . . 12 miles out Fredericksburg Road in 1940s newspaper advertisements. It operated . . . from about 1942 through 1952.

. . . My father's voice, very soothing, masculine. "You were in first or second grade. Remember old Cap Tallmadge? He sued the Texas Rangers!"

. . .Cap Tallmadge," . . . a well-known impresario in San Antonio, having operated several nightclubs before establishing Mountaintop. . . Tallmadge tried to get an injunction against the Texas Rangers, some of whom had removed a loudspeaker . . . during a raid on the premises.

My father drew me back to that mesquite covered mountain. Cap Tallmadge, the top-ranking crazy in a crazy family. He lived on the property in a shack made of milk crates, the heavy kind used to deliver milk in glass bottles, six or eight to the crate. In my ramblings around the 45-acres of Mountaintop, I avoided his so-called home, even though my mother said he was harmless.

"Remember, Speck? We could hear music in the summer, when the windows were open and the breeze was right." I heard the music. Felt the breeze. My father laughed. "It closed for a while. When it reopened, Cap tried to call it a health resort and nightclub."

The new health resort . . . would include . . . amusements and recreation . . . and a pool and a tennis court, but the two-story . . .restaurant and nightclub were . . . the most memorable.

57. By the swimming pool at Mountain Top.

Health resort? I combed the garbage dumps with Cap Tallmadge's kids, Sheila and Freddy, and sometimes we threw empty tin cans at each other. A flying can hit me right above the eye. I ran home bloody-faced, and I scared a good scolding from my mother. I closed one eye when the blood got into it, and I seemed to be running at an angle. Remembering, I put a hand to my eyebrow. The scar was still there – is still there even now. My father took my hand from my face, so tenderly.

58. My mother in front of our cottage with the colored tiles around the door.

"I know," he said. "It bled, but it was superficial. We went swimming the same afternoon. We were allowed to use the pool. And Freddy Tallmadge tried to catch a tarantula on the tennis court. Remember our cottage with the colored tiles around the door?"

The Mountaintop Dinner Club . . . had numerous small outbuildings" on the property, . . .*built for members of Mrs. Tallmadge's family, and . . . Tallmadge Jr. recalls . . . he and his sister Sheila grew up . . . in a house on the property and eating in the dining room, where "Jasper, the cook prepared all our meals."*

We lived in one of the numerous small outbuildings, my father out of work, doing odd jobs around the club in lieu of rent. Cap's wife Margo lived in a bigger small outbuilding, not with Cap in the milk crates. She had blond hair, and paid my mother to bleach it. She didn't tell my father, and a new getaway fund was born, which would later buy three bus tickets.

. . . and the nightclub provided big-name entertainment, including Louis Armstrong, Duke Ellington and Joey Bishop, then a

young comedian who served as master of ceremonies for floor shows that might include song-and-dance teams, magicians and even high-class strippers, such as Zorima the ecdysiast.

Once I was taken to see a show, but I don't remember any big-name entertainment, and there was no ecdysiast. Laughter and innuendo among the grown-ups tipped me off. An ecdysiast probably wasn't some kind of musician, but that's what they said.

I did remember red-headed Barbara who lived on the property for a while, and drove a fabulous yellow Cadillac convertible. She walked around outside in her underpants and bra. Maybe she was an ecdysiast? I know for sure Mountaintop was a place out of time, like a post-prohibition speakeasy, and I ran wild there like the roadrunners and other country kids.

As my father talked, I fell under his spell, loving him again, like I did on Mountaintop. I don't know how many times the phone rang before the spell was broken, but just when I became aware of the sound, it stopped. In the length of time it took to redial, it started ringing again.

I was expected to call my mother at work when I got home from school, and if I forgot, she called me. My father would have known who was calling. "Speck. You'd better answer that."

"Hello," I whispered.

"What's wrong? Why didn't you answer the phone? Were you in the bathroom?"

"No. I . . ." My emotions bubbled over, and I started to sob. My father took the phone.

"Hello, Hazel. This is Dick." A pause. "Dick who? Dick Bagley, that's Dick who!"

I hadn't stopped crying, and yet I laughed, because life is like that. My mother was popular and had a busy social life, so busy she couldn't be sure which Tom, *Dick*, or Harry might be calling. And I realized with glee my father most certainly did not appreciate the humor.

My mental slide show of the past skips forward, and he gathers up his girlfriend and leaves. Before he got to the bottom step, he turned and said, "I love you, Speck. I have to see Tish. I'll always love you girls. I'll be back tomorrow."

59. Me and Tish about the time of my father's only visit. He never saw her at all.

By the time my mother walked home as fast as she could in her high heels, and before the babysitter delivered my sister, Dick Bagley was gone, with a promise to come back. However, see the last line in the divorce announcement? The defendant is ordered to pay to plaintiff toward the support of said two minor children the sum of $100 per month . . . Defendant didn't send it, not once; plaintiff knew he never would.

My mother had an acquaintance from high school named Jim Bell who had become a law enforcement officer. I thought maybe she called him, and he told her what to do, but no. She called reliable Aunt Jackie, who called a lawyer, and the lawyer called Officer Bell. Texas gentlemen had (and still have) a soft spot for *widows* and their *fatherless* children, and before the sun came up again, the Butterfly and her sister with the help of the law had the Bombardier tracked down, arrested, and thrown in the pokey for failing to pay child support. He agreed to leave town forthwith, and was released with the empty promise to send the back child support.

Would I see him tomorrow? Would he see my sister? On graduation night my high school sweetheart, who was always trying to look after me, asked if my father would show up, and what then? Would I hear from him when I married or when I had my first child, his first grandchild? Did he ever love me? Would anyone ever love me? Soon enough I knew in my head that I would be loved, that I was loved. It took longer to know in my heart.

Is it possible to have children and forget them like a catchy tune that fades with time? I don't know, but I know when he got back in the car and drove away down the alley by the Catholic church, the Bombardier was gone.

I never saw him again.

CHAPTER SEVEN

What's Past is Prologue

What's past is prologue. The Tempest, Act 2, Scene 1, by William
Shakespeare

**60. The Danforth Elementary School Choir. All choir photos
in this Chapter are courtesy of Al Mitchell, TCHS Class of '65, who
generously looked through his files whenever I aked him to.**

There's something captivating about a school choir, beyond
the simple appeal of children together, singing. In a town the size of
Texas City, a choir delivers a kind of prologue. The prologue of a play
sets the scene and introduces the time, place, characters, and so on. In
this picture of the Danforth choir, I see the future in the past. The little
singers were a group, a graduating class, and part of a whole
generation which still knows the same lyrics, sings the same songs.

The bows are green satin, though memory is fickle as spring. If Alice told me the bows were red or Dennis insisted they were blue, I'd believe them both. After all, they're in the picture. The photo can't tell the truth; it's black and white, something memory never is.

61. Sharon Maris, first row, first singer on the left.

There's Sharon Maris down front, and my most vivid memory of choir is about Sharon. She had a Botticelli face, and she sang like an angel, too. She sang *I Feel Pretty*, and I never forgot the moment. In a small town the past as prologue is more than a metaphor. It's the literal truth. Sharon sang again at our 40th class reunion, and I was just as impressed.

I still know many people in the photo, and in some cases, better than I did in my school days. Now we are as we were then, but wiser. Our responsibilities have lessened. Our children are grown, and our summers are free again. Instead of just beginning, the urgency of the mating game has tempered to a comfortable glow.

There's a lot of life ahead, but the crazy getting, spending, planning, middle of life is over. For the Danforth Elementary School choir, it was all ahead.

And who was I then? I loved Danforth. It looked enough like a prison to gain my respect, yet the playground beckoned with monkey bars and merry-go-rounds. At last free from domestic turmoil, I was relieved. I was home. I opened my eyes every morning to a new world, with no thoughts nor plans, just a day to unfold as it might, existentialist before I knew the term. I was warped by my parents, as most kids are, one way or another.

My parents' attitude toward children? They thought I was a pet or an idiot, but I was precocious, and I thought they were weird.

62. Danforth Elementary School would have lasted forever if it hadn't been purposely torn down. Photo courtesy of Al Mitchell.

As an example, my father brought home a mutt I named Seven (I couldn't decide which of the seven dwarfs to name him after). Poor Seven sealed his fate by refusing to be house broken. My mother dressed me for a matinée as my father prepared to go out and "meet some people." By the time we got home, my father was back, and Seven was gone.

"Where's my puppy?" I said.

"Ask your mother," said my father.

"What puppy?" My mother's answer left me silenced by my lack of vocabulary, but dear Mom in Heaven: "Do you imagine I didn't know I had a dog in the morning and by afternoon I didn't? ARE YOU CRAZY, LADY?!"

63. Top row, left to right: Alice Bucklew, Mary Jo Cook, and Danise Miller.

In sixth grade I trusted no one but Danise, not adults, not boys, not even teachers, and I had regrets already. I knew I wasn't kind to my sister, but I didn't know how to be different. She was too often my responsibility, and I didn't want to be her mother. I didn't know how, and I wondered who was supposed to be *my* mother? Tish became confused, too, and later she rebelled. Our cross-purposes would take deep root.

Before my mother remarried, I kept house, did the grocery shopping, and minded my sister. My mother did the best she could, and parenting wasn't a verb yet. When I was expecting my second

64. Merry-go-round at Danforth, courtesy of Al Mitchell.

child, my mother told me I was lucky. She tried hard not to have ANY kids, and she took what she got. Wow. Good one, Mom. I feel better about myself now. As with so many things, what hurt to hear then makes me laugh now.

As for my sense of values at 11 and 12 years old, I swallowed the prevailing bigoted bull ca-ca at large, even though TC was probably better than most Texas towns in the '50s. On my first day at Roosevelt, my mother told me to be myself, which was merely useless advice. The first day she sent me off to Danforth, she said, "Don't play with the Mexican kids." This was bad advice, and ignorant.

When we had PE, and I did play with them, I thought they were nice, Francesca and Ruthie and Lydia and the others. Pleasing my mother was paramount, though, so I did as I was told. I regret it to this day, because not getting to know them better was a huge loss for me.

There were a lot of Mexicans at Danforth, and people develop an irrational fear of things as the numbers increase, but there were

65. Ruth Loya.

other groups in the "don't play with" category. I heard whispers about Communists, queers, and colored folks, but that was under control. The coloreds had their own school and their own town. Queers? I thought this meant peculiar, and the whole population of TC could be called peculiar in some way, so I was confused. When I finally understood what this meant, I felt sure we didn't have anybody like that in our town. Commies? Please. The unions at the refineries wouldn't have stood for that! I noticed I was having an appalling number of ideas that went against the wind, but I forced myself to remain mute, to purge any renegade thoughts.

Texas City was my hometown, and I loved it, even though these attitudes were ugly in thought and in practice. You don't love anyone or anything because they're perfect. You take them as they are, and when they change for the better, you're glad about it. The virulent prejudice of the '50s has passed away over time, or at least been diluted.

I soaked up too many lessons from fairy tales, too. *Rapunzel*: good hair is key. *Cinderella*: the right shoes can change your life. *Snow White*: keep house for someone until your prince comes.

Sleeping Beauty: just stay asleep until he gets here. At least there was counterbalance in movies like *Bambi* and *Old Yeller*.

Consider Bambi. His mother is killed by a hunter pretty quick, and eventually his forest home goes up in flames. As for Old Yeller, he saves the family over and over, and Travis loves him, but has to shoot him. Is there a '50s kid alive who ever forgot Travis drawing a bead on the beloved but rabid Old Yeller?

I feel weepy even now. I doubt either of these movies, iconic as they are, would get passed the drawing board in this age of sucking the truth out of anything for kids. Too bad. These films were about life, about coping, about doing what you had to do.

And one last thing regarding who I was in sixth grade. I thought birds flew overhead and bees made honey. By the seventh grade, childhood would be gone, but we were lucky in the '50s. These days childhood is brief, replaced with computers, organized sports, and a proliferation of sexual images and foul language we once wouldn't have tolerated. Computers and sports are good (*in addition to* freedom and outdoor time, *not instead of*).

I can't fathom how children benefit from being saturated with sexual images. I knew nothing about sex until my mother told me when I was 12 years old, and I doubt if I was any more innocent than most girls that age in the '50s.

But I stood on the launching pad of sixth grade. I was an existentialistic, regretful, guilty, innocent, mute mass of self-doubt, like everyone else on the verge of puberty.

Danise and I had a novelty in sixth grade, a male teacher, and although I have a high regard for the profession, he had one strike against him.

He liked to say "look it up" when you asked a question, and I disliked that. I heard that from other teachers, and I went away not knowing the answer and suspecting they didn't either (another thought I didn't express). A strange memory of Mr. Milton: he was so upset when the Soviets launched Sputnik, he cried.

Why? why did it induce him to cry?

The best part of the school day was the milk delivery. Milk was available for two cents a carton, in plain or chocolate, ice-cold, and by now I've eaten everything from Snickers to snails, but I remember that icy mid-morning milk better than the cassoulet I had at the Stein Erickson Lodge in Beaver Creek, Utah, my favorite meal of all time. Perhaps because the milk came with a side order of memory, and all I got with the cassoulet was beans.

66. Mr. Milton, the only male elementary school teacher in town. Photo courtesy of Al Mitchell.

One day Mr. Milton interrupted the bliss of milk consumption by introducing a new student named John. "Can you guess how he spells his name?"

"J-O-N," I gave in for once to the impulse to speak.

"Why, that's right," said Mr. Milton. "How did you know that?"

Then another unexpressed thought: If it isn't J-O-H-N, what else could it be? H-A-R-R-Y?

So Jon arrived, and I thought he was cool. He was more sensible than cool, but he kept this to himself. I love high school reunions. People tell you things. Jon told me he felt as inadequate as the rest of us.

Mrs. Edith Williams also taught at Danforth at the time, and one day she caught me lingering outside a classroom. I had a pencil in my hand, and she asked if I was writing on the wall. I wasn't, but her stern presence scared me, and I gulped.

67. J O N Crenshaw

She thought I was lying, which wouldn't have mattered, except she would become my neighbor when we moved to 17th Avenue, and for years I remained convinced she thought of me as the lying little school kid she caught writing on the wall. In truth, she probably didn't remember the incident beyond the same afternoon.

My life finally had an element of permanence, but my mother considered a lot of it temporary. She had no intention of being single or working outside the home for very long.

And here's a bit of prologue: Her future husband was a seaman, and when he was in port, he stayed at a hotel on Fifth Avenue called the Fifth Avenue Hotel. My mother walked by the hotel every day at the same time he left for breakfast. They discovered this when they started dating, and there's little doubt their paths crossed. He said he remembered seeing her. Charming, but I doubt it.

About this time we moved from the garage apartment to a villa on Third Avenue called the Third Avenue Villas. I loved our

garage apartment, but all the moving when I was a child turned me into a gypsy. I was restless, and as long as we didn't leave town, I welcomed the motion. Also, shortly before we moved to the villas, Danise had moved there. For a while our back doors were not 10 feet apart.

We left the garage apartment because on a blind date my mother met the man who would become my stepfather. Cody was handsome and tall, but she had to overcome her fear of

68. Zane Cody Long by the car, 1960.

bad omens. Cody's birthday, including the year, was the same as my father's.

My mother couldn't offend the Widow Wagoner by having Cody spend the night in full view of her back windows. The villas were more private. Cody was at sea for long periods of time, and because they planned to marry, they wanted to save the money he spent on the hotel. He slept on the couch. My mind never wondered beyond what I saw in this regard.

This lack of awareness was fading, but slowly. There were hints of unknown and forbidden tinglings.

Danise and I sipped Cherry Cokes at Agee's Drugstore down on Sixth Street, and we made a point to sit at the end of the counter, where there was a spinning rack of paperback books with lurid covers. We wondered what those girls with bubbling bosoms were thinking as they stared at bare-chested heroes on horseback with falcons on their shoulders and whips in their hands.

We didn't see the Fourth Avenue bunch after we moved to the villas, but there was David the cute paperboy, and Lonnie who seemed nice but wasn't. There was Mike Zipprian, who followed me around the playground at Danforth, but I didn't get it, and I didn't like it.

Still, the past is prologue. I fell in love with Mike in junior high, as soon as he fell in love with

69. Mike Zipprian

someone else, pretty Virleen. When they broke up, he came my way again, but dumped me in a week. That's romance when you're 13 years old.

I went through a couple more stages of puppy love, but Gene was special because he became a true friend. The summer following

70. Virleen Johnson

sixth grade (if memory serves) I fell for Gene, son of the proprietor of King's Shoe Shop down on Sixth Street. I took shoes there from time to time, and it was amazing how slow Gene did minor repairs. The moccasin didn't get re-laced until he had my phone number. We talked on the phone, and his parents drove us to the movies once or twice. We went to different schools, which made it more fun somehow. He even gave me a ring as a token, and my first kiss, walking across an open field behind the Third Avenue Villas. I reminded him of this at a class reunion, and he pretended to remember, but I doubt it. Our romance was short-lived, yet I couldn't return his ring. My sister flushed it down the toilet, so it was gone forever, like our love.

Gene fell for lovely Jean in junior high, and there was never anyone for either of them after that, but I would spend a lot of time with Gene and Jean in high school, because my high school sweetheart, Charlie, was Gene's best friend (still

71. Gene King

is). Gene took me to a dance, maybe seventh grade, and I met Charlie. I asked him once, did he notice me at all at that dance? I was fishing for something like *Yes. You were dazzling.*

His answer was simple and Charlie-like. "Nope. You were Gene's girl."

72. Jean Haack

In Shakespeare's famous lines – *the past is prologue* – there's a suggestion of inevitability, but I don't believe the future is cast in stone. The materials are put in place long before you're ready to use them, and you can choose what you build. I see the trajectory of life as a series of rising concentric circles, all connected, rather than a straight line. Certain actions have consequences that break your heart. My sister and I were estranged and never spiraled back together before she died. I see my mother passing by Cody before they met and the omen of his birth date, and my crush on Gene turning into something real with his best friend. People, if they meet at all, so often meet again.

And here's a happy result of writing this memoir. I've become better friends with many people, and made friends in unexpected ways. For a long time I've owned and enjoyed a book called *Images of America - Texas City*, by Albert L. Mitchell.

I didn't know Al Mitchell, and when I received a message from him about my blog. I was pleased to hear from him, and pleased at his offer to share some of his photos in a more usable size and format, such as the choir pictures I've used in this chapter.

We became e-mail friends, and I told him where I was standing in a choir photo. He did the same. And there we are, one kid apart, young and green, singing our song forever, not knowing we would enter each other's lives again in a future far away.

The past is prologue.

73. Top left is Margaret Pedroza. Top right is Sandy McWhirter. I'm one row down from Margaret, on the left, and Al's one row down from Sandy, on the right.

CHAPTER EIGHT

Ruby Ella Long and Charles Wesley Benskin

74. The Benskins

Christmas in Brownwood, Texas, 1956. Top row, Raymond Morris, Hazel Benskin, Dorothy "Jinx" Benskin Steiner, Charley and Ruby Benskin holding Bob and Mike Steiner, Ray Morris. Middle, Jackie Benskin Morris, Beverly Morris, Violet Benskin. Bottom, Lynn Steiner, Mary Lynne Steiner, me, my sister Tish.

This is my clan, the Benskins, the kin of Ben, some forgotten Scotsman whose wandering descendants wound up a hundred years later in Texas. It's Christmas, 1956, at my grandparents' house, a year after my parents' split. I'm down front with my sister, high-water bangs and dolls. Everyone's there, frozen in time against an explosion of floral wallpaper.

75. Ruby Ella Long Benskin

When I look too long I see the future, and I wish I could warn them, help them by-pass the common sorrows of divorce and alcohol abuse. Mental illness will come, the drug culture, confused sexuality. Children will be buried, there will be a suicide, and even a murder. It adds up in every family.

When I was young, I saw Ruby Benskin, my grandmother, as a harpy in a hairnet, like a cafeteria worker determined to pile your plate with something green and squirming. When she came to Texas City for a visit, there had better be Dr. Pepper in the refrigerator, or there was hell to pay. She talked a lot about the Lord, and I thought the Lord crafted Ruby and Charley Benskin from the hard-packed, intractable clay of San Saba County. At the moment of creation they looked exactly as they did in old age, drained and done-for, never young, always raving or silent, opinionated, bigoted, suspicious, and stubborn.

My grandfather Charley (as he spelled it) was a study in passive aggression. At my grandmother's vicious tirades, he would turn his back, knowing she preferred the high dudgeon of confrontation. If my parents' marriage hadn't scared the romance clear out of me, my grandparents' marriage, a battleground of misery, would have.

When my mother and her sisters dismantled the house occupied by Ruby and Charley for five decades and more, they found nothing of value, but priceless treasures: World War II ration books. A letter, December 28, 1935, from the Texas City National Bank refusing my grandfather an FHA loan, and asking for $1.50 to cover the cost of the appraisal. My grandmother's driver's license, with an unusual restriction: *with pillow.* My

76. Charles Wesley Benskin

grandmother was only five feet tall, and the issuer of the license felt she should sit on a pillow. Old love letters and years of school pictures, kids, grandkids, nieces and nephews. Telegrams and photo portraits, mysterious and unidentified.

Instead of tossing it all away, my mother and her sister Jinx made a good decision, one I'm grateful for. They decided this cache of memorabilia deserved a scrapbook, 30 years before "scrapbooking" became a popular hobby.

Eventually the scrapbook came to me, because (according to Jinx) I seemed to love it, and because I was the only cousin who was interested. That last part isn't true, but the first part is. I loved the scrapbook, and I resolved to take good care of it. However, the materials, an accountant's ledger and scotch tape, weren't well-chosen for the purpose. After 25 years the scrapbook began to deteriorate, so I decided to digitize the material and produce an album that would be available through the internet to all Benskin relatives.

I worked in the dining room at the back of the house, where it was quiet and there was soft light from the garden window. The task became a ritual as I opened letters, looked for dates, found clues in old photos, deciphered faded handwriting. I saw things I'd never seen, and slowly, 20 years after they were both dead, I began to know my grandparents.

Ruby Ella Long

Ruby wakes up to the sound of her father's sobs. It's dark, but she crawls from the heavy warmth of her bed to the freezing floor. She walks to the door of the room she shares with her sisters, and she sees her father hunched at the kitchen table. A candle is the only light, and he holds a pencil. He writes and sobs, writes and sobs, and then he stops, blows out the candle and goes to bed. He doesn't see tiny Ruby, so she returns to bed and imagines her mother's arms around her, knowing she will never see her mother again.

Ruby's up again at daybreak, ahead of Mary or Lucy Ray, who will make breakfast and set coffee on. Their mother, only 31 years old, is dead.

A photograph rests on a low table, in a black cardboard frame. The family in the photo is whole – Ruby on the lap of her father, John Long, her mother gaunt and wasted with the disease that will end her life. Mary has one hand on her mother's shoulder, and Lucy Ray is next to Archie, the only son. Ruby was four years old then, and now she's just turned five.

Lucy Ray comes into the kitchen, picks up her father's letter, the one he was sobbing over, and reads aloud:

77. The Longs. Seated, Ella and Jack with Ruby on his knee. Standing, Lucy Ray, Mary, and Archie.

"Cherokee, December 8, 1899

Dear Ella,

One month today you left me, and oh how long it has been to me. I sit in this desolate home bowed with grief and Ruby crys "Mama gone to heaven and left us." Oh Ella I feel like I will have to run away but when I look at your poor little children I can't leave them oh what will I do how can I stay here without you."

As tears run down Lucy Ray's cheeks, Ruby cries, "Is Papa gonna leave us, too?"

"No," says Mary.

78. On the back of the photo:
Miss Ruby Long in Chapel, Texas.

Brother Archie deserted the family as soon as his mother was buried. John Long didn't, though he never recovered from his wife's death. When he died in 1915, this was his obituary.

"J. J. Long of Cherokee died Saturday . . . and was buried beside his wife . . . He leaves three daughters . . . Mary, Lucy Ray and Ruby. Three nobler daughters never graced a Texas home. Deprived of a mother's love and care and guidance, with a stricken father, . . .they uttered no complaint, with the courage of a martyr they took up life's work where it was left them by a merciless fate . . . earning a support for themselves and their helpless father, they used every spare moment to improve their talents. Miss Lucy Ray qualified herself for the teaching profession and Miss Ruby recently graduated as a stenographer from a prominent commercial college. Miss Mary has given the best years of a young life in devotion to father and home. Brave hearts, noble souls, every heart beats in profound sympathy and adoration for you and yours."

79. Sam, May 6, 1913. A James Dean look-alike.

Ruby was a stenographer? And a *brave heart, noble soul?* My grandmother? It was shocking to know she wasn't always what she became. I wish I knew what she was thinking in that sassy picture, at 13 years old, her arms akimbo, gingham dress and hat.

She never smiled in photographs, and my mother said it was because she had ugly teeth before she got a full set of false ones. Old photos are full of non-smiling people, and even though it was common to be serious, I wonder how many simply had unattractive teeth before fluoride in the water and regular visits to the dentist became routine.

When she was of an age to be courted, Ruby had two suitors, Sam and Charley. Going through the original scrapbook, I found a letter from Sam, postmarked 1914, in pencil, barely legible now:

. . . *Darling why don't you write long sweet letters like you use to write me. I don't think you love me. I am afraid there is another in the way aren't they kid tell me the truth if you have changed . . .would you rather talk to Charley than to write to me?*

In long sighs as an old woman, my grandmother sometimes whispered, "I should have married Sam." This remark, five children and 50 years later.

80. Handsome young Charley.

Her other suitor was Charley, but I found no letters. Was Sam far away and Charley right there in San Saba County? That's a common reason why one suitor wins out over another, but for whatever reason, Charley won the Ruby Ella sweepstakes, or lost it.

81. Second horseman from the left is Walter Benskin, oldest of the Benskin brothers.

Charles Wesley Benskin

Charley has brothers and sisters aplenty, 13 were born, 11 survived, and times are hard. There's enough to eat, but barely, and the family depends on the game the boys bring home. The older ones get deer, mostly, and the younger ones, like Charley, only a boy, hunt squirrel and wild turkey.

Charley's hunt begins like any other. He's deep in the woods, a long way from town, and a long way from home. Something goes wrong. The gun discharges, and Charley jumps. He doesn't feel anything, so he's startled to see his shredded work shoe, blood oozing around the laces. Now it hurts, badly. He sits down to think, then he acts on what he knows. No one will look for him, not today, and if they do, they won't

82. Charley and Ruby as newlyweds.

know where to start. He sees no smoke rising in the trees, so no other hunters or cabins. The nearest neighbor is miles away.

With his shirt, he binds the foot as best he can and walks, using the gun as a crutch. He walks and walks, through pain and delirium, but he bleeds too much. By the time there's a doctor, he's lucky to be alive, and he's unconscious when he reaches a hospital. When he wakes up, his leg is gone at mid-calf. He's 12 years old.

She was Ruby Ella. He was Charles Wesley. Then they were Ruby and Charley until she died in 1973. They once were beautiful and young. Well-turned out, their hair-dos the height of fashion.

I don't know why Charley became a barber, a profession requiring him to stand all day. He limped, and his stump was painful. I grew up seeing my grandfather's prosthetic leg propped against the wall at night. It was a hollow tube he strapped to his hip and waist. It chaffed,

83. The Star Barber Shop. You can just see a thin barber pole on the lower left, by the screen door. Photo courtesy of Al Mitchell.

and the sores sometimes became infected, yet I never thought of him as a cripple, because he didn't think of himself that way. Perhaps he became a barber because it didn't occur to him there was any reason he shouldn't.

Shortly after they were married, the young Benskins left San Saba County so Charley could go to barber college in Galveston, and after that Texas City seemed like a good place to make a living and raise a family.

Charley opened the Star Barber Shop on Third Street, and my friend Wayne Pearson remembers it. Wayne's mother called and gave Mr. Benskin specific haircut instructions, but the little boy had a better idea. A burr haircut would last all summer, and he could pocket the extra haircut money.

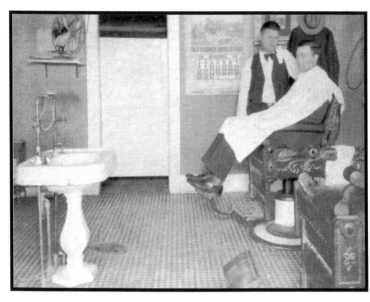

84. Charley in the Star Barbershop.

He showed up alone and convinced Mr. Benskin his mother had a change of heart, and a "burr" was agreeable to her. When Wayne got home, Mom came down like the Inquisition on her skin-head kid, and his plan fell apart.

He was sent back to The Star to confess his lies and apologize to my grandfather. The incident made Wayne so "burr-phobic," he couldn't even bring himself to get a flat top in high school.

85. Young Alex Wayne Pearson on Third Street in TC. Photo courtesy of Wayne Pearson.

Strange but true, I met Alex for the first time in Paris in 1999, and learned he's the uncle of my classmate Sherry Longshore, the stunner I stood next to alphabetically so many times in high school.

Charley was a respected businessman, and Ruby joined ladies clubs, and participated in community theater. According to a newspaper clipping she kept for the rest of her life, Mrs. Benskin gave an outstanding performance in *Bound to Marry*, a Three-act Comedy by Walter Richardson. Other old photos show the Benskins

86. Hazel (my mother), Jackie, Ruby, and Jinx, Easter 1933.

socializing with families called Graff, Pearson, Marshall, and Cross, names still around Texas City when I was growing up.

The Benskin daughters grew up in TC, participating in the May Fete, working on the school paper. Given her community activities, and the pride Ruby probably took in being Mrs. Benskin, wife of the owner of the Star Barber Shop, it's small wonder she didn't want to go down in the 1930 U.S. Census as Ruby "Bruskin." She kept the newspaper review of her performance, and the announcement of The Star Barber Shop, tucked away in her things for 62 years.

The Benskins coped with the Depression, when things weren't easy. Walking with her friends one day, my mother saw her father driving a horse-drawn garbage wagon down Texas Avenue. She waved, but he turned away. He told her later he didn't want her friends to know her father drove a garbage wagon for a little extra change.

According to my mother, even in hard times, Ruby laughed and sang, and enjoyed going around Texas City with her three fine daughters, the Butterfly and my beautiful aunts, Jinx and Jackie. With war on the horizon, the Depression waned and times got better, so what caused my mother to be so miserable at home, so miserable she married to get out? The Benskins were a happy family *before*, my mother told me.

87. Ruby with Charles Wesley Benskin, Jr.

"Before what?" I asked?

"Before the babies," my mother said.

Just as money got a little less tight, and she had more freedom from the responsibility of raising her girls, Ruby became pregnant at 42. And again at 43. Two babies, a peculiar kind of tragedy, because it's also joyful, thus mixing every possible emotion.

This made a wreck out of Ruby. She cried for days on end, and when she wasn't crying, she was screaming at her older daughters and heaping hell on Charley.

In the words of my mother, "She wasn't fit for buzzard bait."

No doubt Ruby suffered from postpartum depression, and maybe a nervous breakdown, with no help nor understanding, and nowhere to turn. Only recently has this disorder even been discussed. In the '30s, my grandmother kept silent for fear her friends and neighbors would think she was neurotic or insane.

My mother accepted an offer of marriage as soon as she got one, and my Aunt Jinx decamped after graduation. My Aunt Jackie had already married, and in photos with her new baby, lovely Jackie looks troubled. Her own mother was physically and emotionally unavailable. The excitement of a first grandchild never came.

88. Hazel and Jinx (in twin dresses), Jackie with Ray, and Fuzzy the family dog.

Charles Wesley Jr was born November 29, 1937. Jackie's son Ray Morris was born March 3, 1938, and my grandmother's last child, Violet Elaine, was born December 22, 1938.

Ruby and Charley had made a good life, beyond what their beginnings might have predicted. They were intelligent and ambitious, and they were successful in the context of the times.

But it was the times that did them in. In 1938, Ruby would have been called insane. Today, she might get the treatment she needed.

Charley either began to drink or began to drink more. Was he an alcoholic? Or did Ruby over-react? If Charley was an alcoholic, he had nowhere to turn either. Alcoholics Anonymous was born in Akron, Ohio, in 1935, but didn't exist across the country until 1941. At the time, heavy drinking was accepted among the menfolk, even encouraged, just part of *boys being boys.*

One way or another, Ruby was relentless. She demanded a geographic cure. Harangued to the point of despair, certainly to the point of capitulation, Charley closed the barber shop.

They left their friends and active social life, and returned to San Saba, a dry county, where folks went to the next county to drink (making drinking and driving a way of life). The only happy times they knew, in Texas City, ended, but the worst was ahead.

The last blow came in 1950. Ruby blamed Charley

89. Violet and Charles, circa 1949.

for what happened, called it the wrath of the Lord for his drinking. But did she wonder, heart-broken, late at night when she couldn't sleep, what part she played in God's vengeance? If they had stayed in Texas City, as Charley wanted, would it never have happened?

My Uncle Charles, playing in the backyard with his sister Violet, followed a ball onto Highway 190, and was hit by a car. Just like that, his story ended. Like his father at the time of the hunting accident, Charles Junior was 12 years old.

This loss was unbearable. Although Ruby lived for 23 more years, and Charley for 32, I don't believe they knew another day of happiness. They over-came many challenges, until the final one that broke them, the death of their only son, and the guilt they must have felt, no matter that it was no one's fault.

When my son Sam was two years old, I took him to San Saba to see his great grandparents. It was a good visit, but what I remember most is one single moment.

90. Ruby, the day her only son was buried.

Charley held Sam for a while, and as he handed my baby boy back to me, my grandfather said, "I had a son for 12 years."

He turned away, but too late. I saw the tears in his eyes.

My Grandparents, Ruby and Charley Benskin, believed in the American dream, and they achieved it. They became better than their beginnings, but it got away from them. Imagine a different outcome. What if Ruby had been diagnosed and treated? Charley might have stopped drinking. And maybe if they hadn't left Texas City, Charles would have played in his front yard on Second Avenue, where the fastest traffic was Fuzzy the dog chasing squirrels.

Ruby and Charley weren't always bitter, old, hateful people. They were ruined people.

CHAPTER NINE

Help Help Me Rhonda

91. The Third Avenue Villas, 1960. From *Images of America – Texas City*, by Albert L. Mitchell.

Twelve-year-old girls in 1958 lingered at the end of childhood, suspended where summers were magic, not so eager to don the feathers and straps of womanhood as they are now. I pushed back at the changes in my body, ignored the wild emotions I had never experienced before. I felt safe with Danise, and safe in our habitat, the wondrous Third Avenue Villas.

Strange, what art evokes. The Musée d'Orsay in Paris has a fine collection of paintings by Henri Rousseau, and I'm fond of that artist. As I stared at *The Snake-Charmer*, something seemed so familiar.

92. *The Snake-charmer*, **by Henri Rousseau.**

What was it, so far from home, so far from Texas? Aha. The Third Avenue Villas, dark and mysterious in the over-grown corners of my memory.

The villas are sad slums now, the once-lush vegetation dead or gone. It's not easy to imagine the wonder-garden it was, unlike anything else in TC. Nestled around four square blocks at the intersection of Third Avenue and Ninth Street, it was a slice of Southern California, oleanders, pomegranates, fig trees, oaks, laurels, and palmettos. Built in 1943, money was miraculously allotted for *landscaping*.

As a priority in TC, and maybe most of Texas at the time, landscaping fell right behind filling in gopher holes in vacant lots. A homeowner might plant sorry-looking bushes around the foundation, and that was it. The word *lush* was too sexy for Texas City.

Lush it was though, in the villas, where Danise and I lived. We wanted everything to stay the same, yet the summer after sixth grade, change infected everything. My mother married Cody, a decent man, hardworking, a good provider. She remained unavailable, immersed in her new husband. This might have caused problems, but he was kind, and my mother's behavior was consistent for the times. What mattered was The Man.

93. My mother and Cody on their wedding day.

Even Danise's mother, gentle and child-loving, withered when her husband was home. We all tread lightly then, so The Mister wouldn't wake up, so his dinner would be on time, so he wouldn't miss the news on TV. All about The Man.

After Cody married the Butterfly, they bought a car, a big Oldsmobile in imitation of my Aunt Jackie. I didn't have to carry groceries from the Big Chief down on Sixth Street all the way to Third Avenue (milk, hamburger, potatoes). Cody, good-natured and accommodating, would drive me and wait while I shopped. He worked as a towboat captain on the Intercoastal Canal, so he was gone for weeks at a time, and although this was hard for my mother – they were insanely in love – it made the adjustment easier for my sister and me. Soon after she remarried my mother would quit her job, and having her home all the

**94. The Villas in 2006. Danise and I sat on the stoop
in the evenings. Sad to see the Villas so run down.**

time - now there was an adjustment that interfered with my daydreaming.

Danise and I stayed outside all summer. We hid among the palms and pomegranates, from our sisters, from the cute paperboy on his manly scooter. Something new was afoot about boys, way beyond the fun puppy love of last season. Still, in the heavy foliage of the villas time would never find us, nor would the paperboy, and we could be little girls forever. And yet . . . the new thing coming was alluring and unknown. We were afraid, either that the changes would happen, or that they wouldn't.

If we needed a billboard for change, we had one. The town itself.

The football stadium at Ninth Street and Texas Avenue, with its open bleachers and chain link fencing, was across the alley from our back doors, and during the fall of sixth grade, we sat outside, listening to the groans and cheers, march music, announcements, honking celebrations as the winners left the parking lot, and cat calls from the losers. It was beyond exciting, even if the Blocker we knew, on the same property as Danforth, had already moved to the old high school on 14th Avenue.

We would start seventh grade at Blocker Junior High soon, and we would be part of it then, but the old stadium would be replaced by a grand one on Palmer Highway.

There was a new high school, too. Texas City High School, Version New, was a surpisingly good example of mid-century modern architecture, all the good parts were there, outdoor patio entrance, good lighting, wide hallways, but none of the bad parts, such as blue plastic siding and cheap materials.

95. Blocker Junior High, October 2006. Torn down now and consigned to memory.

As the town was changing, so were we. We dreaded it; we longed for it. That's what it was to be neither a child nor an adult.

I no longer looked like a brunette Pippy Longstocking. My pigtails were gone, my hair was loose, but I wasn't satisfied. I persuaded my mother to give me an atomic-powered home permanent, so tight I couldn't even wear my Easter hat that year. To add to my lack of sartorial charm, my mother bought my clothes a size too large. She said I would "grow into them." I was almost 13, and I looked like an 8-year-

96. **Fay Kuhn**

old or a 30-year-old, take your pick. I still had a tomboy heart, so I thought it was funny. That was about to change.

When school started, Danise and I took the academic changes in stride. Emotionally, though, something wasn't right. We couldn't go on clinging to each other. We had to find new ways to be, but we weren't ready to let go.

We found new friends like Fay, witty and lively, and sweet-natured Winnie. But our closeness to each other was diluted, and this was happy and sad.

We observed the "popular kids," and wondered how they were different. We became aware of how we looked, and although I didn't yet attach importance to the matter, I realized I had no taste. My mother's style wouldn't work. I knew that much. She loved prints and ruffles. I didn't favor either. I favored – well, I didn't know what I favored. I didn't know what I was supposed to wear, do, say, or be, and neither did Danise, about herself or me, and the distance between us widened.

So puberty arrived and settled in, and once that takes hold, it doesn't let go until it's done its

97. **Winnie Carolyn McGarr**

job, which is to throw things at you willy-nilly and let you make the best of the mess. We weren't doing badly, about normal I'd say, until something happened, an explosion of self-doubt brought on by a catalyst with a pretty name.

Rhonda.

Rhonda's in the Rousseau painting, too, but not the dark, alluring figure, or the snake in the garden of villas. No, she's the flute. She knew songs we had only heard in the distance. Rhonda showed up and played a siren song right in our faces. She caused quite a stir.

She came to Blocker after the term started. I walked into homeroom one Monday morning, and there she was. I had been the new girl in school time after time. I knew she could use a friend, so I spoke to her. She was pretty, but though appearance was on my radar, I didn't obsess about it. It's a shame when that changes, when your face stops being just your face, and your body becomes an object to be scrutinized, then criticized, no longer just the reliable, sturdy thing that runs and jumps and gets tan in the summer.

As I talked to her, I noticed the boys were acting crazy, coming to the door of the classroom, peering pop-eyed at the new girl. The boys acted like idiots most of the time these days, but this was worse than usual. What I didn't process was that at 13 years old, Rhonda had the figure of a well-endowed woman, and she was wearing a tight red dress meant to show it off.

I think about Rhonda now and then, but I don't know who she was, not really. I don't have a photograph, but she imitated her idol, Sandra Dee, and she looked a bit like her, so over time she's become Rhonda/Sandra in my mind. I reached out to her because she was alone and new, but we became friends because her family rented a house next door to Flowers Drug Store, on the corner of Ninth Street and Seventh or Eighth Avenue, an easy walk from the villas.

Rhonda's stepfather was in the military, and military families acquire a sophistication born of travel and of mixing with a diverse group. Sometimes, especially in young girls, it's only skin deep, just a reflection of the adults they live with. Although Rhonda had a know-ing way about her, I doubt if she was more experienced than other girls our age. She was a nice little girl in a grown-up body, and that's a difficult thing to be.

Rhonda started hanging out with Danise and me at the Texas City Teen Club, a good place for kids our age. Located on Sixth Avenue not far from the First Methodist Church, we had fun in a safe setting, ruled over by a devoted gate-keeper, Mrs. Eileen Kirby. There was a jukebox and a dance floor, pool tables and ping pong tables. I met Joe Cross, but I wasn't al-lowed to *car date,* as it was called. My mother said when I was 16, and not before. Until then, my dates and I were sedately chauffeured to the Show-boat Theater by smiling moms and dads. Joe picked me up at the villas once, and my mother de-manded to know if he was driving. He told the truth. He was driving, but his grandmother was in the backseat, a regular old-fashioned *duenna.*

98. A surly 13-year-old wearing just the right thing, fur collar, gray suede loafers, can-can slips.

After the fabulous Rhonda arrived, I still loved the teen club, but not as much as before, because she got most of the attention. She liked to stand out in a room by wearing red, she told me, but I didn't think it was the color of her dress the boys were looking at. I became aware that everything about me was sub-standard. Flat hair, flat chest, pug nose, short legs, you name a negative, I had it. I worked on my hair, and the atomic home permanent was gone, but no matter what I did, it stayed arranged for 30 seconds and never looked like Rhonda's shining blond locks. She once asked me if I had ever heard of hairspray. I had not.

One time Rhonda and I were going shopping. I dressed in my favorite outfit, a black satin skirt and a pink sweater with glitter leaves down the front (it makes me shudder now). I strolled confidently down Ninth Street to her house, but when I got there, she gave me a certain look, a once-over, and I knew. The skirt was butt-sprung, and the leaves that once were gold had tarnished. Why didn't I realize that before?

Rhonda's aunt-who-was-a-model taught her how to dress, wear her hair, apply lipstick for a pouty-look, and even how to stand and walk. I knew standing up from sitting down. Rhonda told Danise and me her *wardrobe* was based

99. Rhonda/Sandra, who tried to steal Jimmy.

on brown. We looked at each other, bewildered. If either of us had such a thing as a wardrobe, it was based on whatever was on sale at Penny's.

My best Rhonda-moment took place as I was coming out of the Showboat after the five o'clock movie, and I met her on the way in to the seven o'clock movie. Her date had a car. My date's parents were waiting at the curb. However, Rhonda wore a blue shirtwaist dress, a white sweater, and black flats. I wore a yellow shirtwaist dress, a white sweater, and black flats. I had got it right!

With 20/20 hindsight, I know it wasn't about measuring up to Rhonda. I didn't measure up to anything, since I didn't know what the standard was. When I first entered seventh grade, I decided to be Beverly, my vivacious, popular cousin. Bev was a *band kid*, so I joined the band, ignoring my lack of interest in music unless it involved Elvis Presley. Most kids took up an instrument in sixth grade, so I was behind to begin with. I was allergic to practicing, I hated the clarinet, and I didn't have Bev's outgoing personality.

I stuck to band for another year, but by the time Rhonda arrived, I had an inkling I couldn't be Beverly. I still had the problem of who to be, though, so maybe I could be Rhonda. I wish someone had whispered in my ear: *Not in a million years.*

Boys liked her a lot, but some of them liked me, too, Jimmy Kickbusch in particular, whose cheerleader sister Jo Ann and her friends ran around the house in shorty pajamas. They thought it didn't matter about "little Jimmy." He was just a kid, and he told me with a grin he wasn't going to tell them any different.

Rhonda called the house one day, but I couldn't talk because Jimmy was over. In twenty minutes she was at the door, uninvited, all blonde perfection, and she made a big play for him, sitting on his lap, stroking his hair. I found the display shocking. It could only go so far. My mother was upstairs, but still. Jimmy didn't mind, but he didn't buy it, either. It probably scared him. She asked him to call her, right in front of me. She had the grace to admit later he never did.

Rhonda wasn't mean. I liked her when it was only the girls around. I suspect she had insecurities, too. Maybe her attractiveness was the only thing she thought she had going for her, and she had to prove something. She was like Jessica Rabbit: she was just born (drawn) that way.

Jimmy moved away before high school, and as preposterous as it sounds, three years later I attended a school function at the University of Indiana in Bloomington, and ran right into Jimmy in the cafeteria. More preposterous, I was still comparing myself to Rhonda. I asked him why he liked me better, even though she was obviously a superior female.

He shrugged. "I dunno. She was Rhonda. You were you. I liked you."

That was the last time I saw him. To this day I wonder what happened to Jimmy. I wonder about Rhonda, too.

But Jimmy's answer caused me to consider how much of my mother's advice I should disregard on my way to becoming a grown-up, such as *don't be too smart, the boys won't like you. Don't beat the boys at tennis, they won't like you.* But what if I was smart? What if I was good at tennis? What if Rhonda could be Rhonda, and I could be me, and that would be OK?

I left childhood behind when I moved away from the Third Avenue Villas, and I left Danise, for a while. Sometime between ninth and tenth grades Rhonda drifted out of my life, too, and from the libidos of the boys in Texas City, but she helped me a lot. Or maybe I learned a lot from what she represented, or from the battle of being neither a child nor a young woman, the same battle she was waging.

Even though I had graduated from high school by the time The Beach Boys released *Help Me Rhonda* in 1965, my mind went right to the only Rhonda I ever knew, the one who set the boys a twitter in junior high, and the one who made a lasting impression on me.

How did Rhonda help me?

If you want to stand out in a room, wear red.

If you want your hair to stay put, use hairspray.

If you want a versatile wardrobe, base it on a single color.

If you want to be Rhonda, forget about it.

My mother gave me good advice in fourth grade: *Be yourself.*

That takes a long time – years and years – but it's the only chance you've got. Be yourself. I learned how easy that sounds, but how hard it is to accomplish.

Here's what E.E. Cummings said about it. It's a beautiful, hard, universal truth:

To be nobody-but-yourself — in a world which is doing its best night and day, to make you everybody else — means to fight the hardest battle which any human being can fight, and never stop fighting.

Never stop fighting. Never. Stop. Fighting.

CHAPTER TEN

Dance Band Challenges

Seventh and eighth grades run together in my memory, all messy and disorganized. Next to an insane asylum, I can't think of anything crazier than a congregation of 13- to 15-year-olds thrashing about in brand new waters, self-conscious, happy and unhappy, terrified. Memories are like fingerprints – no two are the same, but I remember Blocker Junior High, seventh and eighth grades, as one big minefield, a new catastrophe around every corner, coming right at me.

I watched the popular kids to see how they were different. Better-looking? More money for Bobbie Brooks outfits? More self-confidence? I almost decided not to like them, but I remembered: If they didn't know me, I didn't know them, either. Maybe bad things hid under their beds, too. I had read *The Great Gatsby*, and I fell in love with the advice Nick Carraway received from his father: *Whenever you feel like criticizing any one . . . just remember that all the people in this world haven't had the advantages that you've had.*

My own advantages and disadvantages seemed to be one and the same. My mother and father had been preoccupied with mutual destruction; my mother and new stepfather were absorbed in the infatuation phase of love. Thus, they all stayed out of my way. Even as a child, I recognized the advantages of this. I had lots of time to read, and no one questioned what I read. Perhaps I might have made good use of more parental guidance, but then, there's freedom in not being watched too closely.

I didn't know the popular kids well enough to judge them, but I could see the advantages of being popular. I tried things, like pep squad (gray skirts, maroon blouses), but I wasn't a joiner. After school I wanted to be alone and daydream.

The Bombardier said I was pretty, smart, funny, capable, sensitive. Obviously, I wasn't pretty, smart, funny, capable, or sensitive enough for him to take an interest, which left me wondering if there was anything about me worthy of attention. Girls who get abandoned by their fathers have to deal with it, but no one gets out of life without something, and of all the bad things under the sun, that's not so bad. But I didn't trust or understand the attention of boys.

When the spring formal dance came around, I was terrified. Rhonda would be invited by every boy at Blocker, and I would be ignored by all the boys now and through high school, and I would die a young old maid of 30. I was correct about Rhonda, but wrong about my own fate.

Enter Raymond, my knight in shining loafers.

I liked Raymond. He was good-looking and had a cute personality. When he invited me to the dance, I was amazed and pleased to accept. Now I faced the looming disaster girls deal with every time something happens that's special, not special, in town or out of town, formal or informal. I had nothing to wear.

My mother's suggestion made me consider infecting myself with the plague so I could cancel my date. The Butterfly thought I might wear her lurid, low-cut purple divorcée-going-out-dancing dress. An old-lady dress. Please, God, let me die first. Instead, it came to pass I would wear my cousin Beverly's beautiful dark blue gown.

I was thrilled. I had never worn anything like it. Such dresses wore all the girls in 1959. I thought perhaps the blue dress could dance by itself, but for sure it could stand alone. These gowns were constructed in the devil's workshop and given to young girls as torment for original sin. The area where the bosoms went was a cavity, a uni-boob bramble cage.

The dress had a voluminous skirt under which went a big hoop skirt, and the whole thing was wired and re-wired. Lucky it didn't get plugged in somewhere. We all would have been electrocuted.

And finally, it fit Bev, who was a couple of years

100. Beverly in the blue dress. Beautiful. On her.

older, and had something to put in the bramble cage. I tried it on. My poor little lightly padded strapless bra (that I didn't need) left a four-inch cavity.

But hey. I turned sideways and considered my new, hard-wired silhouette. Rhonda-wowza! I looked good! The front of the gown was cut high and camouflaged with little ruffles, but still. How did I imagine no one would notice this miracle, especially my date. The legendary magical thinking kicked in. What could go wrong?

Imagine the big night:

Raymond's mom drives him to my house, and the young swain alights, corsage in hand. My mother answers the door, and I sail into the room like a goddess on a ship's prow, with wired up non-breasts jutting ahead.

Raymond's eyes pop out, but he's no moron. He's navigating strange waters, too, and he stays cool. He probably thinks: "What do I know? Maybe they were there all along. Maybe they did show up between Friday afternoon and Saturday night. Go easy, Ray. Don't let your eyes come out of the sockets and career around the living room."

101. Typical '50s prom dress over-whelming Barbara Hunter and my cousin Jim Benskin.

And then, he remembers: "Oh my God. Mom said I should pin this corsage thing on her dress." The corsage trembles in his grip. He stands in front of me looking anywhere but at my chest. I'm sure he will faint, but my mother snatches the corsage and pins it to the front of the dress. She lines us up for a photograph (alas, destroyed in Hurricane Carla). "There. Run along now. Have a good time." She smiles. She should have laughed out loud.

My date looks like he just escaped a firing squad, and my dress is wearing me. I'm pretty sure a good time isn't on the horizon, not tonight.

Raymond's mom drops us off, and the first catastrophe happens before we get inside. I don't know how to manage the hoop skirt, and I'm wider than the cafeteria door. I try to go through by squeezing the skirt and hoop from the sides. The front of the rig rises up like the hood of a '57 Chevy. I can't see anything but blue, but my panties and garter belt are on display to anyone who's looking. No one told me to wear a half-slip for modesty's sake.

We get through the door, the dress settles down, and Raymond presses his hand into the small of my back. Now the dress hurts, for heck's sake! No one told me to wear a contraption called a long-line bra, either, which would have kept the raw tulle seams from scraping the skin off my mid-section. In fact, no one has ever told me anything useful, beginning with don't ever, ever go to a dance, even if adorable Raymond invites you. Stay home and read "The Great Gatsby" again!

Next, we face Teen Dilemma No. 1: Where to Sit in the Cafeteria. We stare at a room full of pale faces, and spot a table with a few empty chairs. No doubt, the kids at that table are praying someone, anyone, will sit with them, just as we're praying we won't be turned away. We're allowed to sit, and we aren't shooed away. But now we're expected to get up and dance. That's the rule, and Raymond and I are rule-following Texas City kids.

Life as I know it ends after we dance close to a slow number and the empty wire boob-frame collapses inward. Given the layer of ruffles and the dark color of the dress, the newly concave area probably doesn't show, but I speed off to the ladies room.

I lock myself in the stall and push the wire out again. It makes a popping noise. Ha. I push it in and out a couple

102. Uni-boob in bramble cage.

of times. Pop pop. Ha ha. The sound echoes against the tile, and makes me giggle, and I realize how ridiculous it is, and how benign. No one is going to die because of a dress. I do the popping thing a couple more times and laugh out loud. I fill the bra-cavity with toilet paper (it takes a whole role), and I've won the battle. Now back to the war.

I glide up to Raymond and smile. He smiles back. I laugh, and even though he remains clueless, he laughs, too. And just like that, we start to have fun. We talk to each other, and talk to the other kids. We dance again, and the toilet paper does its job. We enjoy refreshments, politely thank the chaperones, and before I want it to be over, the lights flicker on and off, and parents wait in the parking lot to collect us newly-minted paragons of social success. We have survived our first formal dance.

I woke up the next day wondering if Raymond was now my boyfriend, or wanted to be my boyfriend, or if he was off somewhere playing baseball. I decided to reserve judgment on this weighty question. He sat next to me in the clarinet section of the Blocker Junior High band, so I would see him on Monday and figure it out.

I never imagined Raymond would become my nemesis instead of my boyfriend.

I signed up for band because my popular cousin Beverly (owner of the blue dress) was in band. But it wasn't like we were in the band together. She had moved on to high school. Still, it seemed like the right thing, until I took one look at the black-hearted clarinet. Play it? I'd rather beat someone up with it. So I *pretended* to play it. I named the nasty thing Beelzebub, and it was full of holes that meant something to someone, but not to me. The mouthpiece came off so you could empty out the spit. Who wouldn't love something like that?

I loathed summer band practice, which started in August so we could be ready for the sacred football games in September. I don't have to explain Texas City in August to anyone who's ever been there. No trees, no breeze, the relentless sun, and me in a walking nightmare, pretending to play the clarinet. Given a choice, I would have spent the time being run over by a tractor. Being in the band suited Beverly, but it didn't fit me any better than her blue dress.

Once as an exam we had to play a solo in front of the whole band, just a few bars. Did I practice? Well, I *meant* to. But I spent Sunday night at Beverly's after a family dinner, the band solo far from my mind. On Monday I had nothing to wear to school, and no time to go home. I couldn't wear my jeans from yesterday. Girls wore dresses or skirts and blouses.

Bev did her best, and we found two options. The first was a pink dress she hadn't worn in three years. It hit me about four inches above the knees. Her other dresses didn't fit. It was the chest again. Bev had a figure; I didn't. I could show my knees (not yet fashionable) or look like I recently had balloons under my dress and someone let the air out. I went with the knees. The first person I met in the hall on Monday morning, naturally, was Rhonda. She laughed out loud. Time to employ magical thinking again.

I'm hopeful. Maybe I won't be called today. There are a lot of kids, and we won't finish in one day. I can then practice all night, and tomorrow wear something that belongs to me. Band class comes, and Mr. Meyers draws names from a hat to determine who will play. I'm called second. SECOND.

I stand in front of everyone in my short pink tutu dress, put the horn in my mouth, and what comes out can't be called music. I blow a couple more times and start to cry. The whole band jeers and boos (they do no such thing, but I hear it in my head). Mr. Meyers rolls his eyes and says I can sit down. He doesn't ask about my good intentions. I don't feel badly treated. I don't blame Mr. Meyers. I knew about the exam. I should have practiced.

Here's where Raymond re-enters the picture. Musicians, even in junior high, sit in their sections according to their musicianship. The first chair in any section is occupied by the best musician, last chair by the worst. Miraculously, I wasn't last among the clarinets. I was third or fourth from last. Mr. Meyers must have preferred the musicians who played nothing to those who played badly. Playing nothing actually got me moved up a few chairs.

As for Raymond, he was one chair lower on the scale of completely incompetent horn-blowers (I can't go on referring to us as musicians). Raymond found this situation intolerable. Mr. Meyers allowed his kids to move up via the "challenge." The kid below you in the section could challenge for your place, and move up one chair if they won. Raymond just had to do it.

We're assigned a piece of music. For once, I practice. My mother advises me early on to let Raymond win; don't scare the boys off. I just can't do it. When the day comes, Mr. Meyers sits in a room where he can hear but not see us, to avoid any appearance of partiality. One at a time, we squeak away on the bloody clarinet. I win. But Raymond's relentless. He challenges my chair regularly, and I keep winning. I loathe and despise the procedure. I don't understand why it matters who's third from last or fourth from last in the Blocker Junior High band, and yet, I practice every time. I also don't know why I win, unless Raymond suffers from nerves. He doesn't look nervous. And what the hell anyway. To call either of us musicians insults musicians all over the world. By the end of the school year not only is adorable Raymond not my boyfriend, we barely speak to each other.

At the end of eighth grade, I decided to look for something else to be. I was athletic, so maybe I'd run for cheerleader. I tried out on the auditorium stage in front of the whole student body, yelling a silly little rhyming cheer called *Grandpa's Top Hat and Grandma's Bustle.*

I'd rather play the sobbing solo in a pink tutu than stand on stage and do that again. I didn't get enough votes to become a cheerleader. My stepfather legally adopted Tish and me in the spring, so Becky Bagley didn't appear on the ballot, and no one knew who Becky Long was. I have no illusions I might have won otherwise, but this allowed me to feel better about losing. And trying out was something I picked for myself, not because of someone else. Win or lose, that was progress.

The only thing left was to tell Beverly I was dropping out of band. She would be disappointed. I summoned my courage at a family picnic, and blurted out the tragic news. She looked at me like I said I didn't care for the three-bean salad. Whether or not I stayed in the band was a non-matter to her. One more time, nothing that threatened my existence was as bad as I thought. Or else I found something to laugh about, and got on with the process of growing up.

In seventh and eighth grade, I learned to laugh at myself. I learned nothing involving dresses, popularity, clarinets, and other large-looming small things is that bad. I learned if you practice and prepare for about anything, you'll do it better. I learned competition between friends requires maturity. The outcome might not be what you want or expect, so proceed with caution.

103. Handsome Raymond McNeel

At the Texas City High Class of '64 50th reunion, I saw Raymond and felt such a surge of affection for him. I wanted to thank him, but I wasn't quick enough to articulate what I felt, so I'll say it now.

"Thanks, Raymond, for everything. Thanks for asking me to a dance. Thanks for challenging me. Thanks for helping me grow up."

CHAPTER ELEVEN

Carolyn

Carolyn gave me a wind chime, a delicate thing, bought at Rock's Variety Store down on Sixth Street, held together with nearly invisible strands of wire. When I lifted it out of the box, it made a sweet sound, ephemeral and gone again the minute I closed my palm around the hollow tubes.

The light from the Christmas tree in my living room made her face glow pink. She was 14 years old, with freckles across her nose, and soft, curly hair. I envied her curls, but she disliked them – *hated* them, she said. Carolyn at that age hated or loved everything.

104. Carolyn Ann Williams

"It's not a Christmas present," she said. "This is to say I'm sorry. For hating you before I even knew you."

****

105. Carolyn's house in 2006. It looks almost the same as ever.

After my mother re-married, she wanted a house, and in the summer of 1960 her realtor called to say he had a great deal, a house on the south side of 17th Avenue at Second Street. It was no palace, just two bedrooms and one bath, but a good location, and the payments might be lower than rent at the Third Avenue Villas. My mother jumped on it.

A few days after we moved in we were out back hanging laundry, cheerful work, full of the scent of new-mown grass, sunshine, and big, big sky. The breeze off the water a block away whipped the clothes about, making an engaging sound, crisp, musical, almost like a wind chime.

Our new next-door neighbors came out to take the sheets off their line, and my mother wanted to say hello. As we covered the short distance between our clothes lines, I recognized Mrs. Williams.

Uh oh. I had a flashback to Danforth Elementary School, and the

106. My house in 2006. It looks different from when I lived there.

time Mrs. Williams thought I was writing on the wall. To make it worse, she had been sure I was lying when I denied it. I had a pencil in my hand (the smoking gun), after all.

There was a girl, too, but the sheets danced around us, bringing her in and out of view, and only when Mrs. Williams plucked the last sheet off the line did I see the girl clearly. I couldn't think of her name, but she went to Blocker, and she was in the band. She resided at the front of the clarinet section with the real musicians. I sat in the back, battling with Raymond over third from last chair. She played the clarinet better than me, but so would a tree stump if it had lips.

"I'm sure you know Carolyn from school," said Mrs. Williams.

Carolyn clapped her hands with delight (yes, she did) at the happy news I was her new neighbor. I knew it was an act, but my attention was on Mrs. Williams, who at any moment would call me a liar and string me up with the clothes line.

That didn't happen, but back in the house, I was a nervous wreck. Sooner or later Mrs. Williams would reveal my criminal past to Carolyn, my mother, everyone on 17th Avenue and beyond. My mother didn't notice my dismay, but remarked on how nice it was to have a neighbor who liked me so much.

"I'm not so sure about that," I said.

"Well. We'll all go to the beach."

That was the Butterfly's standard and surprisingly effective solution to all social problems among friends and relatives. Who could be up-tight at the beach?

Carolyn and I encountered each other hanging out clothes or bringing in the morning paper, and one day my family was

107. Carolyn in the front yard on 17th Avenue.

heading to the beach. My mother insisted we invite the Williams girls, and after that, Carolyn and I began seeking each other out. Still, we seemed an unlikely pair to become best friends.

There were small but symbolic differences, such as Carolyn needed glasses and wore them, and I needed glasses, but my mother said the specs spoiled my looks, so Carolyn saw where she was going, and I floated around in a Monet painting. Carolyn was grounded and conventional. I was a dreamer, a free spirit, inclined to do as I pleased within reason. After all, my mother was a Butterfly. Carolyn's mother was a teacher, an educated woman, a hard-worker, independent and ahead of her time. Carolyn had lived on 17th Avenue as long as she could remember. I lived everywhere and nowhere. Even in Texas City, this was my fifth address.

On a deeper level we had some important things in common. We were both children of divorce, abandoned by our fathers, leaving us with low self-esteem and a driving desire to please our mothers. We were neither inclined to rebellion. To me it seemed like a lot of trouble for nothing, and to Carolyn it was simply unthinkable. Finally, we were

108. Left to right, Carolyn's sister Eileen, my sister Tish, me, and Carolyn at the beach.

both bright, and we *got* each other. She made me pay attention; I made her laugh.

So we become best friends, and we liked to sit on the swings at the park on 16th Avenue and plan all kind of things. We would spend the night at the new Holiday Inn. We would go to Houston. We would live in Paris. We anticipated high school, just around the ninth grade corner, and we decided to write a book about popularity. We would call it "How to be Popular in High School." How we imagined we qualified to write anything of the kind beats the stuffing out of me.

We spent hours on this project, taking notes, making outlines, until we got into a philosophical dust-up. We agreed you had to be good-looking to be popular if you were a girl and athletic if you were a boy, but it stopped there. I insisted popularity hinged on being just like everyone else, the right clothes, clubs, boyfriends, hair-dos. Carolyn said, no, that wasn't right. You had to be so unique people would flock to your originality. We scrapped the project due to creative differences, but we understood that whatever magic it took, we didn't have it. Not only that, being popular started to seem less important than having a best friend.

109. Terry Boyd

Our most intimate conversations took place in the Green Bean, Carolyn's family car, a green '57 or '58 Chevy, parked in her driveway. It was a private place where we could talk with no possibility of being over-heard.

She hated it when people couldn't remember her name; she felt invisible. It hurt my feelings when people disliked me without knowing me. When I said this she looked like she might even cry.

"This is terrible," she said. "But I have to tell you. I almost died when I found out you were my neighbor. I hated you."

"I knew that. Look at your face in the mirror. You couldn't fool a blind man, not about anything that matters. But why did you hate me?"

"Terry."

"Terry? Like a towel?"

110. The formidable Mrs. Edith Williams (white collar), with the Green Bean. Photo courtesy of Al Mitchell.

She laughed. "Terry in the band. I had a crush on him, and everyone said he had a crush on you."

Ah, junior high love. If Terry had a crush on me, I didn't know it, any more than Andy knew I had a crush on him, and he had a crush on Liz, who liked Robert, who liked Carolyn, who liked Terry, who (maybe) liked me.

Then I made my confession. When we met at the clothes line, I hadn't remembered her name. "So we're even. You hated me without knowing me, and I made you invisible."

We had a good laugh and a long debate about whether it was better to be hated or invisible.

Carolyn felt her visibility problems would vanish when she could drive the Green Bean instead of just sit in it, since the main point of driving in Texas City was to ride around town in circles and be seen. If you drove straight for five minutes you would be out of town, so TC was over-run with circling child-drivers, some barely able to see over the steering wheel. Carolyn took drivers education and became a fully licensed driver, no restrictions, when she was 14 years old. She did become more visible, but not in a good way.

111. Carolyn and me in front of my house, 9th grade class day, May 1961.

Carolyn probably begged for days until we were finally allowed to go out in the Bean. We went wild! We ate French fries and Tiny Burgers (20 cents apiece) at the Terrace Drive-in. I dared her to "drag" the Terrace, which was considered unladylike, but she did it, twice, then pronounced me a bad influence as we roared off down Palmer Highway toward the high school. At a stop light, we pulled up beside some boys we knew, and the boys revved the engine. Carolyn revved back, the light changed, and we zoomed off, reaching 35 miles an hour in under a mile. The boys were long gone.

We weren't bound for anywhere in particular, so we circled back and headed down Sixth Street. The same boys pulled up again. There was smiling and revving, but this time we turned to the right and headed home. We had to be back at a certain time, so we took off for 17th Avenue and landed in a shit storm.

Mrs. Williams stood on the porch with her arms folded across her chest as we pulled in. This was trouble, so I high-tailed it over to my house, praying it had nothing to do with me. In 20 minutes the phone rang, and two minutes after that my mother appeared at the bedroom door.

"Edith wants to see you. What did you two do?"

I didn't know. I knew Mrs. Williams was upset, but we went to the Terrace and road around. That was all, I said.

I trudged next door to my execution. As it turned out, two or three people called Mrs. Williams while we were gone to report that Carolyn and her side-kick were careening all over town, madly chasing after a car full of boys.

This was Texas City. Someone was always calling someone's mother about something, but I honestly didn't know what the matter was this time. Mrs. Williams had interrogated Carolyn, and I was next.

She took me into the bathroom, the only private place in a small house with four other occupants, closed the door and demanded an accounting of our afternoon. I didn't leave anything out, even about the boys. We hadn't raced, and we hadn't chased anyone. I even had the good sense not to say what I was thinking: *As the toilet is my witness, I swear I'm telling the truth.*

My story lined up with Carolyn's, so it was clear our misbehavior had been exaggerated by the town gossips. We got off with a mild scolding, but at least I knew she had forgotten the lying pig-tailed fifth-grader who used to be me. Otherwise, she wouldn't have believed my story.

When Carolyn and I compared notes, we laughed, but we agreed. Telling the truth was the right thing to do. We sure could have dug our hole deeper if we had lied. What a valuable lesson that was.

Interesting people are always full of contradictions, but back then I didn't know that. I was surprised that Carolyn, who couldn't tell a real lie without turning purple, could tell white lies with ease, and quick about it, too. In September of 10th grade the two of us joined Junior Achievement and went door to door selling our product, *Gard-Its*. Who wouldn't want a bag of foam rubber coat-hanger covers, all different colors, and for only one dollar?

We knocked on a door, and the worst happened. The door opened and there stood Gail Sanders, Miss Popular at Texas City High. If that wasn't bad enough, behind her lurked her boyfriend, Diron Talbot-the-Football-Player, best known for standing in the hall at TCHS and barking. Carolyn and I were speechless. And horrified.

"Uh. We're from Junior Achievement," I muttered.

As Diron hulked, Gail was perfectly pleasant, I must admit. "Really? Where do you go to school?"

Oh my God. She didn't even know who we were, didn't know we were her classmates! I was one second short of screaming: Texas City High, same as you, bubble-head!

And don't miss the irony. I didn't know Gail any more than she knew me, and there I was, disliking her without knowing her. Shame on me.

But not in this universe was Carolyn going to hawk coat-hanger covers to these cool classmates, let alone confirm how invisible we were in their cool world.

She didn't miss a beat: "We're from La Marque. Isn't this the Jones home? We're supposed to pick up some old clothes for the Junior Achievement charity drive."

We escaped with our dignity, and we agreed. This answered the question. It was better to be hated than invisible. We attached way too much significance to the whole thing, but good sense doesn't factor in when you're an insecure sophomore.

As further proof of her quick wit, when Carolyn's high school boyfriend, Walter, became a cadet at Texas A&M, he invited her up for a football weekend. Mrs. Williams agreed to go as chaperon, but Carolyn was ambivalent about Walter. She wasn't ready to break up, but she decided to guarantee her good time by taking me along. Walter had to find me a date, and he did, with a gorgeous cadet who had no personality.

There was a football game, a formal dance in the evening, and after the dance we had hamburgers at a local dive. On the way to the car the four of us walked down the middle of Main Street, and

112. Carolyn with Walter Winnette, circa 1964.

around the corner came a herd of cows, running right at us. We scrambled for the safety of the sidewalk.

Carolyn had one of those hoop-slip things under her dress, and when she turned too quickly, it came untied at the waist and fell to the ground, puddling around her ankles. If it had been me, I would have panicked, caught a heel in the mess, and tumbled to the pavement in a pile of ruffles. I would have been trampled to death. Not Cool Carolyn. She assessed the situation and didn't move. She stood stiff as a parking meter, her arms tight to her sides, as the cows ran by on their way home, or wherever they were going at three o'clock in the morning in College Station, Texas.

When it was over, she said, "What should I do now?"

"Pick up your slip," I answered.

Carolyn stepped out of the wire rig as dainty as a dancer, picked it up and tucked it under her arm, and floated to the curb like Miss America. In short, she had the situation under control.

Mix equal parts laughter and tears and you get a bonding agent at any age, but especially in the ridiculous days of junior high. Laugh we did. One day Carolyn's younger sister Eileen had to be at school early, but it was drizzling, so she persuaded Mrs. Williams to drive her the half-mile to Blocker. Mrs. Williams wasn't dressed, but she would be right back, so she threw on her bathrobe and away they went. On the way home the over-worked little Chevy coughed, sputtered, and ran clean out of gas. The dignified Mrs. Williams walked all the way down 17th Avenue from Sixth Street in her chenille bathrobe and slippers, in a drizzle that had become a downpour. Carolyn ran to my house to report this event. She collapsed in my arms, she was laughing so hard.

We laughed more than we cried, but we did cry, too. Carolyn loved her friends, all of them, even me, and she was devastated when a friend of her's was killed in a freak accident. She sobbed so hard I held her tight, and I felt the same pain she felt, even though I never knew the poor dead girl.

****

Carolyn went to college, married, had three children, and became somebody within the business community in Houston. She was Young Businesswoman of the Year, a high honor. She was a person to respect and admire, probably from the time she was born, but certainly from the minute I knew her when she was only 14 years old.

There's a big middle of life that's filled with mating, and children, accomplishment, and aging parents, life events that leave little time for old friends. When that passes, there's the chance to reconnect, a re-gifting of friendship, and I know it would have happened for Carolyn and me.

113. Carolyn Williams, Young Businesswoman of the Year, Houston. Photo courtesy of Eileen Williams.

In 1987 I was in Houston for a family event, and I drove to Texas City. I stopped by to see Mrs. Williams and ask about Carolyn. She lived in Houston, Mrs. Williams said, but she was sick. I should have known by that good lady's grim expression that Carolyn was more than just sick.

I got Carolyn's number and called her. Yes, she was sick, she said, but it was going to be OK. If I had seen her face, I would have known it wasn't. But there were complications, and I didn't go see her. There would not be another chance. She died before the year was out.

I don't have many regrets, but not going to see Carolyn is one of them. She was the person I admired most in high school, and to some degree my moral compass. She taught me how to think in a linear, sensible way. I taught her everyone has a free spirit. I helped her find hers.

Over time I've lost or broken many things, or given them away, but I've kept the wind chime Carolyn gave me. Her memory comes and goes, fleeting and sweet, like the sound of a wind chime. When a person dies young, there's the tendency to turn them into a saint. Carolyn was never a saint. She was a warm, rich human being. I never think of my girlhood without missing Carolyn, and knowing her when we were young is a gift I'll keep forever.

CHAPTER TWELVE

The One-day War

Christmas lends elegance to parties, the lights, the trees, the sparkling ladies in evening gowns. The neighborhood progressive dinner promised to be full of goodwill and champagne. The entire group of 40 couples gathered for cocktails at the clubhouse, redolent with pine garlands and glossy magnolia leaves. For the sit-down portion of the progress, we would dine in private homes in groups of five couples, and my husband and I were pleased to see we knew some of the couples in our group, but not others. Perfect. Old friends and new. A toast, a blessing, and we dispersed. The holiday season in Atlanta, Georgia, was off to an auspicious start.

By the time we reassembled at the clubhouse

114. Christmas 1985, Atlanta.

for dessert my reputation as a trouble-maker, which I had managed to out-run several times, would be solidified forever, and all because of Texas City, my home town.

What could go wrong on such a cinnamon-scented evening? If it can, it will, and it did. At the home where dinner was to be served, one of the women I hadn't met, I'll call her Tipsy, singled me out for scorn as soon as we were introduced. Habitual drinkers rarely stagger or slur, but the deep flush around her collar caused me to suspect she had too much to drink at the cocktail party. Her belligerent attitude wasn't personal; if it hadn't been me in her line of fire, it would have been someone else.

She began to grill me. *Did I work outside the home? Oh, I did? And I had kids? What about them?*

I eased away to another conversational group. With ten at the dinner table, however, I couldn't out-flank her. She sat down directly in front of me.

We were served a shallow bowl of New England clam chowder. "Mmmm. This is tasty," I said. "I like it better than Manhattan style."

"Why would you have a preference?" said Tipsy. "Where are you from, anyway?"

"We've moved around a good bit, but I grew up in Texas."

"I might have known," she said. "Where in Texas? I lived in Houston for two years. Why don't you just tell me where you're from?"

The other guests sensed trouble, and it grew quiet enough for me to hear my inner voice. *This is a social occasion. Behave yourself. Have a sip of wine. Calm down.* "On the coast. Texas City, actually."

"Ah," she said. "The town with the redundant name. I've been there."

Keep it light, I thought. "Well, did you know, it's even possible to live on Texas Avenue, in Texas City, Texas."

With that, the hostess brightly excused herself, explaining that the main dish must be about ready.

Tipsy took a long sip from her wine glass and looked at me with evil little eyes. If there was a note on the scale called sneer, she would have sung her next words. "Texas City is just plain tacky. Nothing special about that nasty place. Bad smells. Hicks. Cowboys. And cowgirls."

"Uh huh. One more remark like that about my home town, and this cowgirl's gonna put you face down in your chowder."

No one thought I was kidding. At that precise moment the hostess came back to the dining room. My threat made her stop too abruptly, but the chicken didn't. The beautiful golden brown bird slipped off the platter and onto the Oriental rug. Our hostess breathed "On no" as the huge thing settled onto the carpet with a pleasant little plop. Joy to the world.

No one knew what to do. The hostess retreated to the kitchen. Tipsy's champagne-induced flush crept higher, until her ears couldn't be distinguished from her red Christmas headband. She was watchful, though. She had the good sense to think I still might be coming for her face.

The primary emotion around the table, I imagine, was *how the hell do we get out of here?* A plate of vegetables was passed around with some dinner rolls, while the hostess, on her hands and knees, scrubbed at the carpet. This sight did not promote polite conversation, so Tipsy remained silent, and so did I. As soon as possible, the group de-camped.

If only I could have kept my mouth shut. If only the damn chicken had stayed put. I waited until the others had gone and made my apologies, but I felt terrible, not about Tipsy, but for our hostess. It's a brave and generous thing to entertain eight people for dinner, and she didn't deserve to have her party spoiled. She was as gracious as possible under the circumstances.

I wanted to skip dessert at the clubhouse, but I made myself go. From the time I stabbed Sherry Anderson with a seam ripper in Home Economics, to the thing in Munich with the gingerbread heart and the high kicks, if I make a mess, I face the consequences. Tipsy, however, didn't show, and in spite of my remorse for our hostess, I hoped I had scared the crap out of Tipsy.

115. Big Vic the Stingaree

But here's the thing. By the time we arrived at the clubhouse, the Battle of the Texas City Chicken was known to everyone, just as it would have been back home, when no matter how small the infraction someone would call your mother. My fancy neighborhood was just another small town. So was Texas City just another small town, too? Exactly like Tipsy said?

If it was no different than other towns, why did I feel such a deep affection for it? Why did I miss it, even though I hadn't lived there in 20 years?

116. Rita/Rati Hughes

Why did I love to talk about Texas City, even though the place requires a surprising amount of explanation? First I have to explain that I didn't say *a city in Texas*. I said *Texas City, Texas*. Most people north of the Mason-Dixon Line have never heard of it, so I explain where it is. Then there's the *Stingaree*. The name of high school mascots doesn't come up often, but it comes up now and then.

"Did you say *stingray*?" is the usual come-back.

"*Stingaree*. It's mythical, like a unicorn. It's sort of an orange stingray, with teeth, and it stands up, and sometimes it has blazing six-shooters. Does that help?"

"Orange? Is it a real animal?"

"Do you expect to win the lottery on Sunday?" I say.

On the subject of nomenclature, as dinner table conversation I've been guilty of telling tall tales, such as only two middle names are legal in Texas City, Jo for girls (Becky Jo) and Wayne for boys (Bobby Wayne). I've explained (more or less) why Rita was called Rati and Terry Fales was called Ferry Tales.

There's also Armelia (not Amelia), and Danise (not Denise). There's Archibald called A-Ball and Dorothy Lee called D-Lee. We had Wey-mond (not Raymond) and Emken Linton, the student, and Emken-Linton, the funeral home. People love this stuff.

I've explained Texas City football and Tackle Time, and

117. Terry/Ferry Fales

that the two have nothing to do with each other. When people see pictures from my class reunions, I explain that, no, it wasn't Halloween.

Then there's the Texas City Dike. Texas Citians over the age of 13 rarely think about the double meaning, but others do. The funniest remark to date came from an openly gay colleague at work.

"The Texas City Dyke? Is that an elected position? I've always wanted to run for office!"

This is quirky small-town-in-Texas stuff, and fun, but none of it explains the loyalty many of us feel for TC, and after the Battle of the Texas City Chicken, I pondered: What made Texas City different?

The answer came to me at the Pentagon in 2003, in the Humanitarian Relief Corridor in the A Ring, which depicts places around the

118. The TC dike always looks the same.

world where the U.S. military has assisted the civilian population. Right up there with the Berlin Airlift, as a part of the permanent exhibit, is a black-and-white photograph of Texas City in flames.

And that's it. That's what's different about Texas City. Before 9/11, no other American city experienced a One Day War.

On April 16, 1947, the port of Texas City suffered the greatest loss of life in an industrial accident that ever happened in the U.S., before or since. The *SS Grandcamp* exploded, followed by the *SS High Flyer*. The cargo: some five million pounds of ammonium nitrate, the combustible material in bombs. This became known as the Texas City Disaster.

The impact of 9/11 compares to nothing else, and yet, comparisons are interesting. The population of Manhattan on that day was 1.6 million, and 2,606 people died at the World Trade Center. That's .16 percent (*point* 16 percent). The population of Texas City in 1947 was 15,000, and 600 people died. That's *four* percent. For the percentage of people who died in Manhattan to equal the percentage of people

119. Texas City, April 16, 1947.

who died in the TC Disaster, the number would have to be 64,000 Manhattanites.

On 9/11, 343 firemen lost their lives when the towers fell. In TC, the number was much smaller, but the entire 27-member volunteer fire department ceased to exist. NYC had a hero mayor in Rudy Giuliani. TC had a hero mayor in Curtis Trahan.

In a town the size of Texas City, the injured and dead were loved ones, friends, neighbors, and the paperboy who biked to the docks to see what was happening. The Class of '64 thought of the Disaster as history, yet to the survivors who were our parents, it would have seemed like yesterday. Consider that 9/11 happened well over a decade ago, though we remember it like it was last week, yet young adults now

120. Jim Bell, Jr.

don't remember that singular day in 2001 in New York, Washington D.C., and Pennsylvania.

And the Texas City Disaster was a One Day War, with the full arc of that most awful of human debacles. The day was perfect, sunny and mild, but something was going on down at the docks. At 9:00 a.m. Officer Bell of the TC police department said that as far as he knew – as far as anyone knew – everything was under control. Fire fighters were on the scene, and no one expected an explosion. At 9:12 the world according to Texas City blew to bits.

Over 600 people died. Thousands were injured. The streets looked like news footage of European refugees wandering through rubble, like something from the front lines of World War II. Veterans of Pearl Harbor said it was like December 7, 1941, when warships buckled trying to ride out the chaos. It was worse than the buzz bombs at the Battle of the Bulge.

Two classmates that I know of, Ricky Lindsey and Carolyn Stork, lost their fathers in the Disaster (Carolyn's dad's co-workers created a fund for her education, and she became a nurse).

What follows is a first-person account of that day from my cousin, Ray Morris, who was in third grade at Danforth Elementary school.

121. Carolyn Stork

I remember seeing a huge, black cloud of smoke with flames at the base. I thought the Japanese had bombed us again. We were taking a spelling test when we heard a loud explosion. We looked at the windows where the sound had come from, and then the glass shattered, cutting all of my fellow students to some degree. The students close to the windows were cut the worst. I had a little cut on my ear and on my eyebrow.

We filed out like we were having a fire drill, the teacher saying "don't run." I still had my pencil in my hand, and I thought, "I don't need this." I dropped it. We ended up in the playground, in a daze and sobbing. Mom found me and gave me a big hug in relief. She said "if we find your dad alive, we are getting out of this crazy town and never coming back." I remember the large amount of debris on Sixth Street as we headed home. We were living in Snug Harbor. Yet, even that far from the explosion all of the nail heads

122. My cousin Ray Morris, about the time of the disaster.

were exposed in the walls. We headed for the little airport to spend the night.

There was shock, death, injuries, and destruction, followed by un-

123. My Uncle Raymond Morris, air traffic controller for a day.

certainty. Who was alive? What friends and neighbors were gone without warning? And then human beings did the best they could to cope with the aftermath. All in one day.

My cousin's home five miles away was unsafe, so his family stayed with the Donahues, owners of a municipal airport, not much more than a couple of dirt runways. The next day my Uncle Raymond, an ordinary citizen, became an air traffic controller. He stood in the middle of a muddy field directing airplane traffic as the National Guard and Red Cross all tried to land at the same time.

The people of TC experienced extremes of grief, post traumatic stress, and then the process of healing. Even the fact that there was no way to tell black body parts from white body parts had an impact. Amid the overwhelming tragedy, people wondered what difference it could possibly make, and they were all buried together. The memorial service for the dead was open to all races, and this was remarkable in Texas in 1947.

Social change is a lengthy process, but once people allow themselves to think even for a minute that skin color might not matter, the hard resistance becomes softer, more penetrable, and in 1963, when

African Americans integrated Texas City High School, there was barely a shrug.

The Disaster had an incalculable effect on the citizens of Texas City. Our parents survived a war, and they were never the same. People noticed something about Mayor Trahan when he came home after World War II, and I think it applies to TC after the Disaster.

It was the same thing that they had seen in other men who had come back after surviving something immensely cruel, elemental, and furious. His sense of ease was now almost wholesale. His volcanic tendencies were gone. Curtis Trahan was a steady man. He had the glow of a good man who really had denied death its dominion. (From *City on Fire,* by Bill Minutaglio.)

124. Mayor Curtis Trayhan. From *City on Fire***, by Bill Minutaglio.**

Texas City didn't become paradise. It had its share of pettiness, nosiness, bigotry and narrow-mindedness, but the One Day War changed the temperament of the town. Europeans in the 20th century understand war. When it's all over, they will say folks become gentler, more patient. They know life is fragile. They hold tight to what matters and let unimportant things go. They love their children better. I don't know how long it takes for the memory to become abstract and the post-war effect to dribble away. Maybe only a generation. But long enough for the children of the survivors to grow up in an environment of kindness that engenders an exceptional loyalty to their home town.

Now, when I'm asked where I grew up, I go directly to the Texas City Disaster. People are astonished to learn that in 1947 in a small Texas town 600 people were killed, and 2,000 were injured. Neighborhoods were flattened, and school children wandered among the body parts on Sixth Street. A major industrial plant nearly vanished. Just as 9/11 changed everything, April 16, 1947, changed everything in Texas City.

I think that's why, at a dinner party in 1985, I ignored personal insults and a snotty attitude about Texas, yet I couldn't let Texas City go undefended. I know why I would do it again. I owe that much to the generation who cared enough to call our mothers when we stepped out of line, the generation who survived the One Day War, the generation who understood what matters, and understood how quickly what matters can be lost.

CHAPTER THIRTEEN

Dating, Butterfly Style

After high school gradua-
tion, I worked for NASA, and I
went out with a guy from work
who originally came from
London, charming accent and
all. I lived in Houston then,
and from time to time an old
boyfriend from Texas City
showed up unannounced, to
see me or Gloria, my roommate. The Brit was an
engineer, an educated man,
successful, a real grown-up (I
was 18), but still. I expected a
little push-back at this parade
of old beaus. I asked him why
he took it so calmly.

**125. Gloria Moseley,
my friend and "roomie."**

"I know a gentleman when I see one," he said. "The young men
from Texas City, at least the ones who come to see you and Gloria, are
obviously gentlemen. No need for anyone to be rude."

His attitude was positively British, but the idea of the "Texas City gentleman" appealed to me. I would have pursued "Philosopher" as a profession, but to this day I've never seen an ad saying "Philosopher Wanted." Alas, philosophizing remains a hobby, and the philosophical question posed by the Brit was this. *What makes a gentleman, whether they come from sophisticated London or down-home Texas City?*

The engineer was right. I knew that. The boys I dated from Texas City were gentlemen. From what I observed, the other boys at school behaved themselves, too. I double-dated quite a bit, and the boys who went out with my friends, all gentlemen.

That's what I remember best about Texas City boys. They were unpresumptuous and well-mannered. They were gentlemen.

It was a time when girls who behaved like ladies were treated like ladies, so a component of being a gentleman then was respect for ladies? It's just a question. The word *woman* versus *lady* has become politically incorrect, and I wouldn't turn back the clock on the progress of women, but in certain social matters, I'm not so sure the next generation of women got it right. Young women today can enjoy all the freedom they want and still be a lady, and that's the right and proper thing. What seems to be missing for some, though, is the freedom to say *no* without explanation or apology.

Did being a gentleman mean knowing the rules, not only your own, but those of others, and respecting those rules?

Under the watchful eye of the Butterfly, I began my dating life, and the boys respected the limits set by me and/or my mother.

In the spring of ninth grade my mother pronounced me grown up enough to date, beyond talking on the telephone and being driven to a dance or a movie by parents. My unsettled early childhood made me more mature than girls who grew up in cozier nests, plus because of my November birthday, I was a year older than many of my classmates. I was going on 16 in the spring of 1961.

I was thrilled! It wasn't that I couldn't wait to go with boys. I just couldn't wait to *go*. An action verb. I liked boys, liked their conversation and their company, but the prospect of going any place at all made me tremble with anticipation. Everything seemed like an adventure, and key to this was the car. I didn't care what kind of car, as long as it got us where we were going. Boys had cars or access to cars. Most girls didn't. Even after I got my license, I was rarely allowed to use the family car.

Then my mother spelled out the rules.

Butterfly Rule No. 1: Don't get pregnant.

Don't get pregnant? I was dumb-founded.

How could riding around with boys in cars make me pregnant? When I was 12 years old my mother related the appallingly mechanical *facts of life*, but this wasn't that. Like many small town girls, I was emotionally mature but naïve. Did my mother leave something out in Butterfly Sex Ed 101?

It took me about three

126. Robert Norman and me, Senior Night on the Town.

dates to sort this out. The strong pull of the full moon combined with the privacy of a car and two healthy young people could lead to trouble if you didn't watch out, alright. As far as the fine young men of Texas City, I'm sure while sitting at home watching TV they respected this rule. I'm not sure how they felt after 20 minutes with a girl in a car. Or if they thought about it at all. But then, they weren't afraid they would get pregnant.

Butterfly Rule No. 2. Home by 11 o'clock.

I was invited to Senior Night on the Town in 1962, and I told the young man I had to be home by 11 o'clock, so did he still want to take

127. Young historian Al Mitchell.

me? He did. A gentleman doesn't withdraw an invitation because the rules don't suit him.

Al Mitchell, quite a knowledgeable Texas City historian, tells me the picture of Robert Norman and me resides in the TC Museum. When Al sent me an electronic copy, I didn't recognize myself. I zoomed in (ah, the digital age), and realized it's me for sure. I'm wearing my mother's crystal necklace and earrings, a set she loved. Thanks, Mom. For a lot of things.

Butterfly Rule No. 3. No going steady.

This rule suited me, whether my mother knew it or not. Was I just a baby Butterfly? Even in 1961 this was a shocking idea, one I didn't want to think about, philosophically or otherwise.

No, not going steady suited me because shortly after my parents' divorce, I asked my mother why she married my father in the first place. I wouldn't know the full story of the Butterfly and the Bombardier until 45 years later, but my mother dropped a permanent bomb in my brain with her answer.

"Well. He wasn't abusive *before* we got married."

Boom in my head, and a new guiding principle slithered up out of the brain rubble. No one puts a ring in my nose or on my finger, friendship, wedding, or otherwise. Before I ever heard the term "fear of commitment," I had it. Many girls went steady, sometimes for a long time, sometimes forever, and it worked out well for them, but it wasn't for me.

I expected Rule No. 4 would be a restriction on frequency of going out, but it wasn't. I could go out as often as I wanted on weekends (no school nights), as long as it was with different boys. Too much

128. The Texas Theater, which wasn't as popular as the Showboat. Outside on the right is the ticket booth; the popcorn machine and candy counter are visible inside. Photo courtesy of Al Mitchell.

time spent with one boy – now that was trouble. Trouble, which starts with T and rhymes with P, and doesn't stand for pool, as claimed by *The Music Man*.

I was new to the dating world when I met Rex Bell at the roller skating rink, and he was a perfect example of a guy who had the undeserved reputation for being a bad boy. His older brother was a bad boy who knocked over the 7-Eleven store on the north end of Sixth Street and did time in Huntsville prison. In TC stuff like this rubbed off on family members, but before Rex asked me out, he told me about his brother. If he hadn't, someone else would have. There he stood at the skating rink, trying to look off-hand and tough, not realizing there's never been a boy born who could look tough wearing roller skates.

"People don't like me because of my brother." He looked away, shy, embarrassed, and adorable.

On our very first date he took me home to meet his mother, a kind lady who gave us Cokes and brownies. Rex taught me to drive a stick shift in the ugliest car I ever saw, a maroon Studebaker with gold hubcaps hand-painted by him. He taught me to play the guitar, too, placing my fingers gently on the frets. I refused to trim my pretty nails, and he shrugged. "You won't be any good on the guitar if you don't." I learned enough to play a folk song or two, but I had as much talent for the guitar as the clarinet. In a word - none.

129. Rex Bell, 1961.

My classmate Armelia dated Rex's friend, Bill Haire, Class of '63. I liked Armelia (and I *loved* her hair). The four of us went to the ninth grade prom and out to eat afterwards, chicken fried steak, gravy, biscuits, all for a dollar, and no calorie worries when you're young and active. We had a great time all through the summer of 1961.

When Armelia fell out of love with Bill, he was heartbroken. I ran into him down on Sixth Street, and he offered me a ride home. We sat in his car for a few minutes while he poured his heart out about his lost love. I commiserated and gave him a hug. By the time I got home, Rex had called a dozen times. His buddies had reported seeing his girl (me) *making out* with Bill. *What?*

I set Rex straight, and as soon as I hung up, Armelia called. Her friends had reported in, and she assured me it was alright with her. I convinced her I would love to have her hair, but I didn't want her ex-boyfriend, and he didn't want me. Small towns.

Rex was smart, funny, talented, and independent. When I wouldn't go steady, he said OK. He would date other girls. No problem. True to human nature, I didn't like that part, and if the Butterfly had relaxed her rule, I might have relaxed mine, but she stuck to it.

Rex brimmed with *joie de vivre,* and he found school intolerably boring. He drove too fast, hung out at the pool hall, and once parked his car up over the curb and onto one of the grassy rings in the TCHS parking lot. He cut too many classes and was about to flunk out, so he joined the Navy early in 1962. We were too young for the relationship we might have had if he had stayed around. Rex had a huge personality, but he was a gentleman who didn't smoke when I asked him not to, and when he taught me to drive he never lost patience or yelled. When I said no (or yes), about anything, I had the last word.

130. Armelia Nelson

In the early '60s dating was uncomplicated and innocent. And inexpensive. Many of the most fun things, like the beach, were free. Gas cost between 11 and 18 cents a gallon, and movie tickets cost a dollar. The girls were polite and kept in mind that popcorn and candy cost extra. We looked at the prices on menus before ordering too much. Gifts might be an Everly Brothers record or a stuffed toy, or for Christmas, maybe a silver charm from Hetherington's Jewelry down on Sixth Street.

By *innocent* I don't mean no one fooled around. Normal human beings are hard-wired to fool around. Some kids went *all the way*, and maybe some were ready for that. I don't know who did what with whom, and I wouldn't say if I did. Most of the boys claimed they "did it," but the rules of chivalry applied. They didn't name names. OK, sometimes they did, and such a specific claim caused people to think less of the boy. It was ungentlemanly. Naturally, the girls said they didn't "do it." I believed both stories, did and didn't, but the purpose of dating was for young people to get to know each other, and it was a process that took time.

Fred Tooley from the Class of '64 sent me an astonishing bullet-list of memories, some 162 of them, such as French fries at Bostick's, wooden floors at Rock's, Hi-Fi consoles, returnable coke bottles, iodine and baby oil, Spoolies, shower cap hairdryers, wooden tennis rackets, but my favorite was "Galveston dates on Saturday night."

Like the magic days of my childhood, in Galveston it's always summer in my memory. The breeze, the clean smell of the ocean, the sounds – seagulls, surf, and the cheerful patter of Bongo Joe, beating his painted oil drums down by the pier.

There was putt-putt golf and a stretch of concrete down on the northeast end of the island where cars could be driven up and down the sides of a paved embankment. We rode the Bolivar ferry and rented bicycles-built-for-two.

I liked to sit in front so I could steer, and I loved to run the thing between the white concrete benches and the edge of the seawall. One guy jumped off after we cleared the narrow strip and swore he would hitch-hike back to TC before he would get back on the bike with me driving.

I loved the beach. There wasn't a movie I didn't want to see. I loved to dance, I loved to eat. I loved the old wooden roller coaster, and I cried when they tore it down. There was swimming and sunning, and going in groups in two cars, so you could close a blanket between the doors and the doorframes to make a shade tent between the cars. I loved the tiny transistor radios you couldn't hear more than two feet away.

**131. Galveston. I loved to steer the bicycle
between the white bench and the drop-off.**

There was a Tilt House, a walk-through attraction with a simple premise. The house was built at an extreme angle resulting in illusions that defied gravity. Angled floors and walls made it appear as if water flowed uphill or a broom stood upright on an angled floor. Everything about it made me laugh.

I loved the beautiful movie palaces like the State and the Grand, and I loved exploring the old fortresses built to protect the island from German U-Boats, Fort Crockett, Fort Travis, Fort San Jacinto.

132. Fort San Jacinto

When I think of the boys I dated, I'm so proud of them. Not only were they gentlemen, they behaved like men, not little boys. Sure, some drank, caroused, got in fights, but even so, my sense of it is, there were limits.

I dated one or two bad boys who didn't last when I found them out. Kenneth from La Marque, funny and good-looking, needed to be watched, and I sensed that. After a few dates, he said it would be him and only him, or he was done with me. I said OK, we're done. No hard feelings. When he drove me home I accidentally left my sweater in his car. The next night he doused it with gasoline and set it on fire in my driveway. I guess he had hard feelings. I only regretted the loss of the sweater.

The boys who were willing to date me on my own terms didn't say *I love madly*, or *you're so wonderful*. They said *you're a good sport – you always have a good time.* Thus I learned that if you want others to have fun, have fun yourself. I had a wonderful time, and I think my dates did, too. They were gentlemen by nature, by raising, and because being ladies and gentlemen was an important value then.

I had a carefree good time between 10th and 11th grades, and then the inevitable happened. In junior year I fell in love, and it changed things. But that's another story.

CHAPTER FOURTEEN

Carla – Hurricanes and Heroes

Tuesday, September 5, 1961 – A tropical storm forms off the coast of Honduras.

Labor day passed, the picnic baskets were put away, and the first day of school arrived. For me this was always a celebration, but especially in September of 1961, my first year at Texas City High School. The heat lingered, but the mood shifted overnight. Time for new clothes, new classes, and football. September,

133. By the car on the first day of high school, September 1961. Tish was a fifth-grader.

134. Endless hallways at Texas City High School.

glorious as summer, but busy instead of lazy, focused instead of dreamy.

Sunshine pounded the treeless patio of TCHS, where I waited with my friend Carolyn for the first bell of the first day. We pretended to be nonchalant, complaining about the heat and the early hour, but excitement bubbled in conversations all around us.

Wow! Our high school has a swimming pool! You were up at 6 a.m.? Me, too! Judy's wearing a darling skirt. When's the first football game? Will I survive PE so early in the day? What about my hair? Five minutes between classes! Can we make it? Where's the annex? Which way is the gym?

The school spread like an amoeba over six acres of flat land in the middle of town, four long wings lined up like soldiers, flanked by the auditorium and the gym. It opened in 1957, so it still smelled new, and the whole town was proud of it.

Wednesday, September 6 – The tropical storm reaches hurricane strength as it moves north past the Yucatan peninsula. It's christened Hurricane Carla.

By Wednesday I knew where all the restrooms were, and I had enough paperwork to read until I was a senior. Everything there was to know about classes, drills, gym clothes, pep rallies, PTA meetings, clubs, student parking, and more. If it existed in the well-established world of public education in Texas City, I had a handout about it.

Thursday, September 7 – Hurricane Carla skims the Yucatan peninsula and enters the Gulf of Mexico.

On Thursday my hair was, in female parlance, a mess, but I couldn't help it. I heard Carolyn honking the horn of the Green Bean in her driveway, so I had to go or we would be late. I only got turned around once that day, when I thought I was going toward the gym, but I ended up back on the patio.

Friday, September 8 - Hurricane watches are issued for the entire Texas coast.

By Friday I was a seasoned high school girl. Carolyn knew where to park. I knew I could sit in my boyfriend's car in the parking lot and still hear the first bell. I had to dash to get to class in five minutes, but it could be done. I felt smug and grown up. Come Monday, no doubt, I would walk around looking as self-assured as the juniors and seniors. What could go wrong?

135. Carla looked something like this. Actual images of Carla are of poor quality, nothing like the digital images available now.

When there's a storm in the Gulf of Mexico, coastal dwellers watch and wait. My mother picked me up from school on Friday (saddle shoes were on sale at Penny's), and after shopping we drove out on the dike as a lot of others were doing. This storm, still 400 miles out to sea, already shoved the tide a foot above normal. It was big, too, with gale-force winds covering an area 500 miles in diameter.

My mother shook her head as she looked at the water. "Too high." She was a Texas City native. She had seen storms come and go, and she didn't like it.

When we got home Aunt Jackie called. She had been to the dike, and she didn't like it either. Tomorrow, Saturday, they were taking my cousin Beverly back to school at Sam Houston State College in Huntsville, Texas. This would serve as their personal evacuation plan. Jackie suggested we come with them in our own Oldsmobile (their Oldsmobile was full of Bev's things). If we had to we could make do and all stay in Bev's dorm room overnight. It would probably blow over by Sunday at the latest.

Saturday, September 9 – The Texas and Louisiana coasts are under a hurricane warning. By 1 p.m. Carla picks Texas, but it's a long coastline. Where? Tides are already two to three feet above normal.

This hurricane's a tease, too, stalling, starting, stalling again, but it's expected to make landfall on Sunday, September 10.

My easy-going Uncle Raymond seldom made demands, but no matter where we were going or why, he always strongly insisted we leave at 4 a.m., which made everyone in the family crazy, but this time it put us ahead of the highway chaos. By noon on Saturday cautious people were leaving the coast voluntarily, before the authorities issued a formal evacuation order. We were already in Huntsville.

Not that everyone complied with the order. As usual many didn't, but during the next two days half a million people evacuated the coastal areas, the largest coastal evacuation in U.S. history at the time.

We avoided the traffic jams, but nevertheless, Huntsville was full of returning students and parents who thought they might as well take their kids back to school a little early, just in case. No matter the warnings and predictions, no one expected a catastrophe until it couldn't be denied. Our plans went south as the storm headed north. There was a mix-up, and Bev's dorm wasn't open for students yet. Every motel room in Huntsville was taken, and all of them had waiting lists.

Raymond (who directed air traffic after the TC Disaster) had five females in his charge. There was my Aunt Jackie and my cousin Beverly, my mother, my sister Tish, and me. Raymond was a Texas City gentleman, and he took this responsibility seriously. There were other men in the family, but my cousin Ray was away in the Army, and my stepfather Cody, a towboat captain, was pushing barges up the Mississippi River.

After trying several motels, all with waiting lists, Raymond got tactical. He smiled and nodded politely, and asked the motel manager if it would be OK to sit and read the paper and wait. *After all*, said Raymond, *I have nowhere to go, and five women waiting in the car, one of them just a little girl*. The manager shrugged. About an hour later, someone checked out. Raymond got the room, waiting list or not. He didn't threaten or bribe. He didn't insist. He just found a way.

He was a hero to me, even though it was just one room with two beds and a small couch. Poor Raymond, the only male, got the couch. Fatigue and worry did us all in, though, and after watching the bad news on TV for a while, exhaustion overtook us, and we slept uninterrupted, even by our nightmares, until early Sunday morning.

Sunday, September 10 – Hurricane Carla stalls, then begins to move and stall, move and stall, and by noon, the storm is 160 miles from Galveston.

**136. Dashing Dan Rather made a name
for himself during Hurricane Carla.**

The next morning and throughout the day, the adults were glued to the TV. A crazy young reporter and former student at Sam Houston State College stood outside in the wind and rain in Galveston. In 1961 the image of Dan Rather in hurricane-force winds, right in front of the Seahorse Motel, was new and riveting. He even waded into the surf to deliver ominous news. Instead of moving inland and dissipating, Hurricane Carla had stalled again. The storm by all predictions would move inland on Sunday, but it didn't. Even with sophisticated weather techniques, hurricanes are ever unpredictable. When Carla decided to move again, it was by fits and starts.

Monday, September 11 – Hurricane Carla finally moves inland at Port O'Connor, 160 miles from Texas City and well within the 300-mile swath of the massive storm. Hurricane force winds and high tides pummel the coast, from Port Aransas near Corpus Christi to Sabine Pass on the Louisiana border.

Bev and I woke up early to find the adults hadn't gone to bed, but stayed glued to the television all night. The storm had moved inland at last, so everyone assumed it would soon be over at least, bad as it was. Dan Rather

137. Galveston, September 1961. Note the relative size of the car and the wave.

spoke of 15-foot tides and 40-foot waves.

The storm dropped from Category 5 to Category 4, but to make up for it, it stalled again, pummeling the coast with 150 mile-an-hour winds and gusts up to 175 miles per hour. Carla danced in circles off the coast for three hours, and the damage multiplied, as if to send a message to all coastal dwellers:

There, said Carla, *you like living on the coast? You like the water, the gulls, the beach, the fresh breezes? Well, there's a price to pay, so pay up.*

And pay up we did. Hurricane Carla did $2.5 billion worth of damage in 2014 dollars. Forty-six people lost their lives.

The rain had pushed inland ahead of the storm, and it was pounding outside our motel in Huntsville. The adults didn't look up when Bev and I donned our plastic raincoats and left the room. We sat down on the soaking wet furniture by the swimming pool and cried. Rain pocked the pool surface and ran down our plastic-covered arms. The hood on Bev's raincoat had a tiny visor, and I can still see the drops falling off the visor onto her cheeks like a '60s love song. *Is it tears I see, or is it rain?*

"That's it." My cousin gathered her composure. "I'll go home with y'all. I can't register for school. My parents will need the money."

I had nothing to offer or give up, though I wanted to. She looked like a hero to me. She would do what she had to do.

138. Texas City, Sixth Street at 13th Avenue, on or about September 12.

We wandered back to the room, and Bev relayed her decision to her mother. Jackie listened, thanked her, and said what mattered was Bev's education, more than carpet or furniture, more than the whole damned house, if it came to that. So Aunt Jackie was my hero, too, and Bev stayed in Huntsville.

Tuesday, September 12 – The storm loses its punch as it moves further inland, but still causes havoc across Texas into Oklahoma, up through Missouri, and Michigan, finally blowing itself out as stormy weather in Canada, ending its 13-day career as one of the most destructive hurricanes in U.S. history.

We were all numb, and I don't remember how long before we headed home. We followed Jackie and Raymond, but we became separated in traffic, and my next recollection is sitting outside at a burger joint in La Marque, a town just across the railroad tracks from Texas City. The little burger place was miraculously dry and open for business.

139. Many roads looked like this when we snuck back into TC.

We couldn't get back into TC yet, and all the motels were full (there weren't many).

My mother didn't know what to do next. That's when she spotted the only person she had ever met who lived in La Marque. He was driving out of the burger joint parking lot, and she ran after his car, arms waving, screaming "Bob! Bob! Stop! Stop!"

I thought I would perish with embarrassment – Butterfly's aren't meant to run – but I didn't understand what a break this was for us. No rooms were available anywhere, and Bob never hesitated. He and his

140. Melba Bradshaw,
17th Avenue neighbor.

wife put us up for days, fed us, and made us feel welcome, and we hardly knew them. They were heroes.

The authorities blocked the main arteries into Texas City, but everyone knew the back way and went home as soon as they could, even though it was terrible judgment. Hazards littered the town. There were downed trees, mud slicks, twisted wires, and boats gone loose from their moorings. We got home and it was bad, bad for us and for all our 17th Avenue neighbors, like Mike Peveto, Melba Bradshaw, and Jim Bell.

Our house was built three feet off the ground, but it was a block from open water. Four feet of water and mud had swirled through our house for days. Every bit of furniture was piled against the walls in the direction of the mighty water, and I couldn't believe the power of such a thing. Nothing upholstered was salvageable. No water or electricity. The receding water left four inches of mud behind. We heard slimy things. The Butterfly broke down. I got to work.

I waded through mud up to my knees and found a bit of garden hose protruding from the mud. I tugged until the hose made a

141. Mike Peveto,
17th Avenue neighbor.

sucking sound and came free from the muck. With an effort I drug it to the garage. The water supply was contaminated, and it gushed muddy and brown when I turned on the hose and washed the muck from the concrete garage floor.

We found usable candles, lit them with my mother's cigarette lighter, and sitting on damp lawn chairs in the shelter of the garage, we ate beans out of a can. We did what we could, and went back to Bob's house, swinging over to 21st Avenue to see about Jackie and Raymond. We found them side by side on the floor of their home, scooping up mud and debris. There wasn't much to say. They were staying with friends at night, and we were still staying with Bob, but like us, Jackie and Raymond came back to their house every day.

It felt beyond peculiar to stand in my living room wielding the garden hose over floors and walls, wooden furniture, even the hems of dresses hanging in the closets.

142. Boats broke their moorings and ended up in front yards. Such a boat lived on 17th Avenue for a long time after the storm.

I don't remember how long the power was out, but it was weeks, and we worked on without it. We put furniture in the sun to dry or pulled it to the curb, heavy with water and mud. I was strong, but I had never done that kind of physical labor, sun up to sun down. Our neighbors did the same, though no one knew when it would be hauled away.

My mother and Cody spoke over Bob's telephone and agreed. He should stay on the river. We needed his paycheck. Almost all our furniture was ruined, including the appliances, washing machine, stove, refrigerator. Done for.

We ate at a Salvation Army soup kitchen, elbow to elbow with the mayor and everyone else, and we got fresh water off trucks going up and down the streets.

143. After Carla. This may be a Chelsea duplex. Photo courtesy of Al Mitchell.

My mother finally managed to have mattresses delivered, then we were home to stay, damp and damaged as it was. The piles of soggy belongings at the curb grew higher all along 17th Avenue and all over town, and we worked and worked. I was the organizer, my 10-year-old sister did what she could, and my mother tried to get over the shock of seeing so much of her life destroyed. The Butterfly wept again as she fished our family photographs, liquefied, every one of them, out of a bottom dresser drawer.

The Williams' family next door had returned, and so had the sun. There followed a period of spectacular weather, sunny, warm, and dry. Carolyn and I sat on her porch and shared what there was to eat, then we went back to work, she with hers, me with mine. Every day there was progress, but for months we walked on wooden floors that felt like old-fashioned wash boards. The dampness dissipated some with the sunny weather, but the smell of pluff mud and dead fish lingered clear into spring.

We heard incredible stories from those who didn't evacuate. A classmate, Faye Pinte, had a stubborn father who refused to leave, subjecting himself and his wife and daughter to a terrifying ordeal. They spent the hours during the heart of the hurricane in a boat in their garage. The rising water lifted the boat to the rafters, and as the wind howled relentlessly, they weren't sure the roof would hold. Faye thought they were going to die.

Bill Haire (Armelia's former beau) came by my house in a pick-up truck, looking for ways to help. His home was among the

145. Bill Haire, TCHS Class of '63.

lucky few that didn't flood. He asked what he could do, and my mother assigned him the worst task there could be, which he did willingly and with his wide smile in place. He cleaned out our freezer full

144. Another of Al's photographs.
Typical front yard decor after Carla.

of rotten, stinking meat, closed up in the heat for days. Bill was a hero that day.

Dennis Black's home near Third Avenue and Third Street was dry, but many of his friends had a foot of slimy mud in their homes. He followed meandering trails in the silt at a neighbor's house, and found water moccasins holed up in a closet. He shot at them with a .22 rifle. I don't know what's scariest about that, the snakes, the gun, the mud or Dennis. Or Dennis with a gun in the mud.

146. Dennis Black

When there are TV shows about the most dangerous hurricanes in history, sometimes Carla is mentioned, sometimes not. After going online for information, it seems to me the media prefers pretty visuals over accurate stories. The old footage from Carla appears crude and uninteresting compared to the high-tech images of later storms, but here are a few facts about our own Hurricane Carla.

Carla shows up as No. 9 on the old Saffir-Simpson evaluation scale, that ranks storms primarily on maximum winds, which may be isolated. This scale doesn't consider size and scope of a hurricane's wind field. There's a newer ranking system called the Hurricane Severity Index (HSI) that assigns points to a storm based on size and intensity, encompassing sustained winds. In the HSI, taking everything into account, it isn't Katrina at the top, nor Ike nor Andrew. It's Hurricane Carla.

November 1961 – Sunny, temperatures well-above average on the Texas coast.

School started again. I believe it was late October, but the sun was out as it was the week after Labor Day, the first week of school, the week before we ever heard of Hurricane Carla. Instead of excited first day chatter about trivial things, this time we remarked on the wet seat cushions from the auditorium laid end to end in the sun like big square fish drying for the winter. We asked each other, *how bad was it for you and yours?*

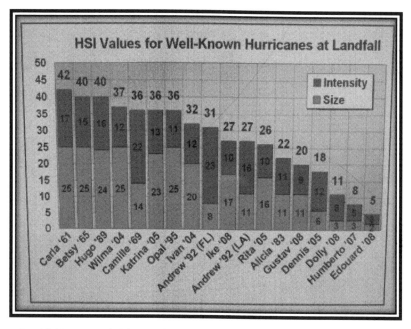

In 1961 my neighbors, friends, and relatives, all ordinary people, met the challenges of a destructive hurricane. When I see pictures of bad storms in more recent years my heart goes out to those who lost so much, but I have mixed feelings. Some of the photographs show homes still derelict, full of mud and debris five, ten, even 15 years later.

There's been a cultural shift in attitude since 1961. I don't remember people crying about Hurricane Carla for years and years, or abandoning anything. Texas Citians were happy for the limited help we got, but we expected to dig ourselves out from Carla. We cleaned up and moved on. That was America in the '50s and '60s, and that was our hometown.

147. TCHS Auditorium cushions drying on the patio.

The Class of '64, raised by survivors of the worst industrial accident in U.S. history, entered high school on the cusp of the worst hurricane in U.S. history, and graduated on the heels of a national tragedy. Our first week of school terminated in Hurricane Carla; our senior year started with the assassination of President Kennedy. Were we better prepared than some for the calamities of the future? We were born to it, weren't we?

After all, the symbol of Texas City is the Phoenix.

CHAPTER FIFTEEN

CaBeLiLa

148. Texas City Logo on a merry-go-round in Paris.

In the last year of the 20th century I lived in a beautiful apartment in Paris, a gorgeous city. I was miserable. It's a Champagne city, and I'd had too much. I hated my job. It was January, and my family wouldn't be joining me until spring.

I ended my day by walking from the American Embassy in Place de la Concorde, where I worked, to the rue jouffroy in the 17th arrondissement, where I lived. Even when it was a bitter day, I often stopped by the merry-go-round in Parc Monceau to see the stagecoach go by. How the Texas City sticker got on the back of it, I never found out, though I tried. I'd been in Paris since September. I wanted to be in Texas. I wanted my family. I wanted my boss to check himself into a mental hospital.

149. Paris apartment.

When I got to my apartment, I hardly had my raincoat off before I booted up my computer, sure I would have e-mail from my husband, my daughter, and maybe my mother, too. I was very, very lonely.

You've got mail, my PC chirped in a new and thrilling voice, a voice that would go from unique to cliché in a few years.

I brightened. Three family messages. Several others, what we now call spam. The last e-mail came from an unknown address, but when I read the subject, I let out a *whoop.*

Subject: *CaBeLiLa*

I knew what it meant and who it was from, or at least one of two possibilities. It couldn't be from *Ca.* A breath of sadness came and went for Carolyn, who died in 1987. The *Be* was me, Becky. So the e-mail had to be from *Li* or *La.* Linda or Lana.

I hadn't heard from either of them in years. Before the internet maintaining friendships over time depended on physical proximity, and we had gone our separate ways a long time ago. With the internet and a little effort, reconnecting was possible. When I felt lost and far away, an old friend reached out across distance and years. It couldn't have come at a better time. I opened the e-mail. It was from Linda.

Warm-hearted, generous, fair, daring, bossy, darling Linda.

A scene passed through my heart much faster than it happened in my head.

I was back in a classroom at Texas City High School in the fall of 1962. I had my back to the windows, as we all did. Mr. Birkner thought the traffic on Palmer Highway distracted us, and taking into account we were teenagers in history class, I'm sure he had that right. I sat up front, with Linda across the aisle on my right. She liked to laugh, often, loudly, and with a crinkly gamine grin that suited her small stature.

150. Mr. Birkner

Mr. Birkner failed to see her charm or mine. We were two warts on his scholarly butt. He had *spoken* to us twice since class started, but when he turned to the blackboard, I whispered something to Linda that made her laugh. She got so tickled she sneezed, and the explosion sent an oval button the size of a human thumb flying off her coat. It bounced once and came to rest between Mr. Birkner's legs. I led the chorus of laughter as he peered at the turd-like thing on the floor. He didn't see the humor.

He narrowed his eyes, extended a bony arm, and pointed toward the door. Linda, all phony devil-may-care, shrugged and gathered her things.

Then he looked at me. "You, too, Miss Long. Out."

For both of us, being kicked out of class was a first, and we had no plan. We could skip school for the rest of the day, but neither of us

151. Mrs. Morton

had a car, and cutting out on foot lacked panache. Besides, she had a GRA meeting later (Girls Recreation Association), and I had an algebra test. She loved GRA, and I would rather wade through alligators than take one of Mrs. Morton's notorious make up tests. She made them extra hard to encourage her students never to miss school again, and especially not algebra class, for any reason, ever.

We settled our backs against the lockers to wait for the bell, pretending not to give a hoot. In truth, we both gave a really big hoot. We prayed Mr. Casal, the Vice Principal, wouldn't pick this hallway to patrol today.

Many of our teachers favored Casal Roulette, that is, kick the troublemakers out of class but don't send them to the office. Let them stand in the hall waiting. Mr. Casal trolled in search of miscreants, and when he found one, let alone two, they were taken to the office and punishment could escalate. We were lucky. The bell rang, and it was now a tale to tell. Wait until Lana and Carolyn heard about this.

152. Mr. Casal

All alone in my far-away apartment in France, I revisited that incident and read Linda's e-mail again, savoring every word. She brought me up to date, told me how she found my e-mail address, and asked about my family. I tried to remember the last time I saw her. Was it 1966? Could it have been that long?

And why did I feel such strong emotions at hearing from her now? It wasn't about being lonely. It was about Carolyn, Linda, and Lana, my friends when I was young. And about *CaBeLiLa*.

Carolyn, first among equals, smart, focused, friendly, charming, self-aware and self-critical, sometimes a little jealous.

For all that, Carolyn's droll sense of humor drew me to her, and being neighbors made it easy to become friends. She was more sociable than I, with a wider circle

153. Lana Hustedde, hair by Linda.

of friends, and early in junior year she brought Linda into her orbit. I came with Carolyn, and Lana came with Linda. We became a quartet.

When my daughter, Shannon, arrived in Paris, I told her about the

154. Linda Chandler, hair by Lana.

e-mail from my friend, and showed her both their pictures in the yearbook (yes, I took my yearbooks to Paris).

Shannon laughed.

"What's so funny?" I asked. "They're beautiful!"

"Yes, they are. But their hair. It's identical."

I knew the story. They lived a few blocks from each other in a part of town called Wayside, and Linda walked to Lana's house on "picture day" to fix each other's hair. Exactly the same way.

Shannon asked about Lana, and I told her I had answered Linda's e-mail at once, and we were in touch, but she didn't have news of Lana.

Long-legged and glamorous, intuitive, intelligent, defensive, lovely Lana.

I last saw Lana in 1989. I attended the 25-year reunion of the Class of '64. She did not, but I looked her up while I was in town. We spent

155. The "Big O"

enough time together to understand we were still friends. We talked easily, speaking about kids, homes, good things and hardships, things we did, places we went. We laughed about the "pink fink," a black panel truck that once belonged to Linda's dad. The four of us, CaBeLiLa, decided to paint it pink, a decision we never implemented, but it was the only vehicle we could depend on having access to, so we loved it.

The Fink took us to Elks Club dances, and to dances in Alvin, where an odd-looking singer with thick black glasses sometimes performed. His name was Roy Orbison, and he recorded *Crying* in 1961, so he was known, but when he recorded *Pretty Woman* in 1964, he became a true pop star and stopped appearing in Alvin.

After any performance of The Big O, we were all ready for the Alvin Stomp, a preposterous dance involving lines of six to eight teens linked arm in arm, careening around the floor trying to knock each other unconscious. We thought it was fun, in a combination football, bumper cars, break-neck kind of way.

As seniors Lana and I took Gregg shorthand, then typing to transpose our notes. Despite the phenomenal efforts of Mrs. Scruggs, Lana spoke Sanskrit better than she took shorthand, while I thought the little squiggles were pretty and easy. However, my typing looked like I used my feet on the keyboard. Every other word was garbled. Lana, though, was a typing fool. Our plan? We would hire out as a team. I would take notes, read them to her, and she would type them up.

156. Mrs. Scruggs

Mostly we used our class time to discuss dating dilemmas, which could account for the unevenness of our office skills. One afternoon Lana couldn't wait to tell me about the fight she had with her boyfriend. She told him never to call her again.

"I was so mad! He asked how he was supposed to talk to me if he couldn't call me. I screamed at him! Send me a telegram!"

Halfway through class someone knocked and handed a telegram to Mrs. Scruggs. For Lana. From him. He would pick her up at seven o'clock on Saturday night. So it all worked out. They got married while she was still in her teens. Then it didn't work out, and they got divorced.

When we met in 1989, Lana's two daughters and her second husband moved around in the background, impatient for their mother's attention. It was dinner time, and I was aware my visit was unplanned.

But we couldn't stop remembering. She walked me to my car talking about the time we crashed the swimming pool at the Seahorse Motel in Galveston. Carolyn, Lana, and I splashed around trying not to get our hair wet, while Linda did something tricky off the diving board. She swam up underwater and pinched two of us before we

157. The Seahorse - gone now.

could get away. We shrieked and made a commotion. The more fun we had the louder we got, and we shortly drew the attention of a motel employee.

He stood at the edge of the pool wearing khaki pants and a white shirt with a Seahorse logo. He gestured until ignoring him became impossible, then he cupped his hands around his mouth.

"Are you girls guests of the hotel? May I ask your room number?"

I sputtered. Linda disappeared under water. Lana saw something fascinating in the sky and stared straight up. Carolyn, however, answered with a perfect mixture of impatience and scorn. *How dare you* dripped from her tone.

158. Mrs. Jarrell, TCHS French teacher, Carolyn, President of the French Club, and Melba Bradshaw.

"Of course we're guests. Room 121." She sighed broadly and began to make her way to the side of the pool. "Just let me get the key. I'll show you."

"Never mind," he said. "I believe you." He couldn't be sure he wasn't pissing off a guest, and it was too much trouble to check it out, so he decided to let it go.

I whispered, "Wow, 121 is your house number!"

"Well, I know that," said Carolyn. "And he's the Seahorse's butt!"

159. Linda, left, in print dress, with the TCHS yearbook staff.
Left to right, Gail Sanders, Vicki Van Houton, (top) Judy Holcomb,
Sherry Anderson, Elizabeth Cranston, and Dolores Geaslin.

Linda cracked up, and we all started laughing again. Mr. Seahorse looked over his shoulder, but he didn't come back. Carolyn suspected he might, though.

"We should definitely leave now," she suggested. That girl could parry a situation like nobody else.

Lana and I shared as many memories as we could in that short visit in 1989, but I didn't see her again for 15 years.

My mother once told me a pleasure of growing older was remembering the past. Not dwelling on it; just revisiting people and places that made you happy when you were young. She was right. After I saw Lana in 1989, I thought about *CaBeLiLa* often, and so I did again when I got the e-mail from Linda ten years later.

When Lana and I met after so many years, what chemistry allowed us to relate as though no time had passed? And would it be like that if the three of us saw each other again? Linda's e-mail opened the door to renew our friendship.

But what did we ever have in common, then or now?

Our interests didn't line up. Linda and Carolyn joined clubs, but not the same ones. They were on the "college track." Linda's picture is all over the yearbook, usually (but not always) dressed for something sporty. Carolyn appears in the yearbook, too.

160. Linda on the right, rockin' a TCHS standard-issue ugly bathing suit.

Lana and I? Nowhere. Neither of us could be bothered to do one thing we didn't want to do in any given moment, and going to meetings – *participating* – was at the top of things we didn't want to do.

Besides, we were apparently on the "get a job" track. I was so oblivious I didn't even know there were two tracks.

Carolyn detested physical exercise, and Lana didn't crave it. I loved to be outside and moving, and so did Linda. A few years ago I had cause to ask Lana if she could ride a bike. She said even though she wasn't an *athlete*, she could *walk* without assistance, and *yes*, she could ride a bike.

Linda and Lana had bonds going back to grade school, but Linda was Daredevil No. 1 and I was Daredevil No. 2. We egged each other on toward bigger risks than we should have taken. Carolyn and Lana held onto our coattails to see we didn't go too far. Linda and I were competitive, and if we had been boys, we might have engaged in fisti-cuffs now and then, which would have horrified Carolyn and Lana. Lana was glamorous. Carolyn was smart. But Lana was also smart, and so was Linda. And Lana wasn't the only glamour girl in the group.

So we were cute enough to get by and smart enough to carry on a conversation. We had to talk to each other, after all, in order to make each other laugh.

And there it was. We made each other laugh.

If we were bricks, that was the mortar. We shared a huge sense of the ridiculous. When we got together we never stopped laughing, and not just girlish giggles – genuine laughter at the absurdity of it all.

We grew into accomplished women with different capabilities, but laughter makes for lifelong friendships. Linda's e-mail in 1999 led to the resurrection of our friendship. We stayed in touch, and when our 40th reunion rolled around, I sent Linda an e-mail. Would she like to meet at the airport in Houston, rent a car, and drive to Kemah to-gether? She would. Should I try again to get in touch with Lana? I should, and I did.

Lana had a high-paying job for the biggest law firm in Houston, with a fancy title and someone else to do her typing. I had recently retired from the State Department in Washington, via Paris, France. Linda owned property all over Salt Lake City and was running her own business. If nothing else, we would all have work adventures to share. I got in touch with Lana, and our on-going series of three-way e-mails began. Lana filled us in on Carolyn's accomplishments, and how she became Young Business Woman of the Year in Houston.

In September of 2004 the three of us sat down together for the first time in 40 years. We met in Kemah before the reunion and began the tradition of drinking a toast to Carolyn, to CaBeLiLa, and to the renewed friendships of the TCHS Class of 1964. Something special was happening for our class, and it's gotten better and better.

161 - TCHS Class of '64, 40th Reunion.

In my maturity I value three things in others. A sense of humor, intelligence, and courage. I generally settle for any two out of three, as long as one of them is a sense of humor. In our green and tender years, I knew these friends of mine were smart and funny. What I didn't know about was their courage.

I don't mean bullet-stopping, flame jumping, charging the enemy courage. Linda still rides motorcycles and she was once on the United States Skydiving Team. Get that? She jumped out of perfectly sound airplanes just for fun. Lana and I are still in awe of that, but that's not what I mean.

The courage I'm talking about lies in coping with life and keeping that sense of humor. Life handed the three of us plenty. The details of our various trials don't matter for these purposes. The truth is, every human being encounters adversity. Those who don't never try anything, never take a single risk, and that's the worst calamity of all.

162. Friends 40 years later. Standing, me and Lana. Linda seated.

When I was young, I thought everybody measured up, did what they had to do, made the best out of whatever life delivered. Time has shown me it's more rare than I thought. The world is full of cry babies, but none named CaBeLiLa. Carolyn, dying young and leaving three children, one only a baby, faced her death with grace, joking with her nurses; her mother told me that. I know of Linda's challenges, and Lana's, and how they stepped up, so now I admire them as well as love them, and we know each other better than we ever have.

We've been friends again and still for ten years and counting. We see each other once or twice a year, and travel together when we can. We go to our class reunions if possible. True to our rascal past, when

Linda visited me in D.C. we crashed a secure area of the Pentagon and were escorted back to the public area between two husky Marines who had the same sense of humor as Mr. Birkner. That is, none. If Mr. Birkner from 10th grade History had been there, he would have tossed us in the Potomac River in hopes Mr. Casal would row by.

We're leading worthwhile lives. We love people who love us back, and we've done interesting, rewarding work. Between us and counting Carolyn, there's seven kids and five husbands. Kids last forever, husbands not necessarily, but friendships? When they stretch out over a lifetime, you've got something to treasure.

I'm lucky to have known Linda and Lana when we were girls, and Carolyn. I'm lucky I still know so many who graduated from Texas City High School in 1964. We speak a common language; we have a common experience.

I know these beautiful souls, all of them, and I'll know them until the laughter finally stops. A long, long time from now.

CHAPTER SIXTEEN

Gangs and Grocery Stores

163. An old photo of the Big Chief grocery store showing the Beeler-Manski clinic next door on the right. Photo courtsey of Al Mitchell.

"Yup. They hang out in the parking lot of Big Chief. I seen 'em."

Thus spoke Johnny, seventh grader and object of my fifth grade affection. I made no reply. I had lived in Texas City for less than two years. Johnny lived in TC all his life. Given his age and experience, he should know, and he said Texas City had a gang called the Red Coats, and they hung out in the parking lot of the Big Chief grocery store.

He expected me to say something, I could tell. I had a thoughtful look as a child, but it was a trick of countenance. I thought nothing at all, unless it was along the lines of *Oh, dear, what do I say now?*

For once, I thought of something. "What about Weingarten's? Do they hang out there, too?"

"Naw. Too far away from Texas Avenue. They hang out at Big Chief."

From the time I moved to the neighborhood around Fourth Avenue and Ninth Street, Big Chief Grocery Store on the south end of Sixth Street was my most frequent destination, not counting Danforth school.

164. Oh. So that's a tuna.

On one of my first visits to the store, I stood at the meat counter clutching a grocery list scribbled out by my mother. The butcher, who looked Italian to me, smiled.

"You want a tuna?"

"Yes, please."

"Little girl, do you know how big is a tuna?"

He walked me to the canned goods aisle and handed me a flat little can. "This is what your mother wants. You need a truck to take home a tuna."

My face burned – at that age I took myself pretty seriously, but the butcher was kind, and that's my overall impression of Big Chief. Kind and friendly.

If I wasn't shopping for my mother, I hung out at the magazine stand by the back entrance, sitting on the floor with a *Superman* comic book on my lap, and no one ever shooed me away. I kept an eye open for foot traffic, but one time I didn't scoot out of the way fast enough. A cross-looking fellow didn't see me hunched over my comic book.

He caught his foot on my ankle and lurched head first into the magazines.

He stayed on his feet (barely), and I expected to be in trouble. Instead, the store people fussed over me and shot looks at the poor man. The store folks recognized a drunken sailor when they saw one, though I did not. There were a lot of bars on Texas Avenue between the docks and the grocery store, and even if Big Chief was the original

165. Weingarten's, courtesy of Al Mitchell.

destination, many lonely seafarers "dropped in" at seedy places before they got to the store.

By the time Johnny informed me of the gangs in the parking lot, I knew about the unsavory characters from the docks, and I supposed a gang was a possible.

I was familiar with the other grocery store, Weingarten's, at the other end of Sixth Street, and it didn't surprise me that no gangs found it convenient or accommodating. It was a chain store, well-lit and modern. Danise's mother piled all the kids in the car every week when the specials came out, and we drove from one store to the other, buying the sales at Big Chief, then the sales at Weingarten's. Gas was cheap and distances were short. And it was fun.

The Miller's had a scary new black-and-white Ford, and it had too much dignity for kids, who might dribble or barf in the back seat, and who sometimes laughed so hard we sneezed or worse. In the old car, we were allowed to enjoy our treat, a six-ounce bottle of Coca Cola, one apiece. In the new Ford we clutched the shapely glass bottles, unopened until we got home. The old car was Big Chief; the new car was Weingarten's.

Johnny had one more thing to say, of great importance, judging by his tone.

"You know what? As soon as I can find a Red Coat, or anyone who knows anyone in the Red Coats, I'm joining. I wanna be in a gang."

He sped away on his black bicycle. I didn't understand boys, and I suspected I never would. What was the big deal about finding a Red Coat? I knew exactly where to look, because he just told me. The parking lot of Big Chief. Did he suffer from memory loss? At 14?

166. Something like the Miller's new car.

I never heard about a gang except from him, and in Texas City there was no chance of keeping secrets, so how could a gang escape the notice of the omniscient grown-ups, who (I was sure) would have put a quick stop to such a thing. The Red Coats existed because Johnny said so, and from then on the pretend games of the Fourth Avenue gang changed.

Sometimes the boys were fire fighters, policemen, or soldiers, and Danise and I became girlfriends of fire fighters, policemen, or soldiers. Our role models were confined to nurse, teacher, secretary or housewife, and as crucial as those occupations were and are, it was hard to fashion adventures around them. To be fair, the boys never pretended to be civil engineers, accountants, or machinists.

If Johnny hung around, we had to be "bad guys," like Jesse James or Al Capone, who in my mind looked like the nice butcher at Big Chief. Mostly we pretended to be Red Coats. We circled St. Mary's Church on our bicycles, backtracked to Hastings grocery store, and tore into the parking lot in formation, twisting the hand-grips of our

167. Hastings grocery, courtesy of Al Mitchell.

"motors," which was the popular moniker of motorcycles in those days. We went inside to buy beer (root) and cigarettes (candy). I wasn't allowed to go to Hastings for groceries. My mother said the tiny convenience store was too expensive.

Bobby had a comb switchblade he bought at Rocks down on Sixth Street and Johnny owned a pair of sunglasses, so they were cool. We pretended to knock over liquor stores and steal cars, but we assumed the main thing this gang did was wear red coats. We turned red sweatshirts inside out to hide the Mickey Mouse logos. By sixth grade, at the tail end of my infatuation with gangs (and Johnny), I found a red coat! A red corduroy jacket, anyway, on sale at Penny's. I didn't say anything about gangs, and my mother bought it for me.

By the time school started and I was in junior high, kid stuff was behind me. I had the red jacket, but it disappeared from the gym and reappeared on a brazen ninth-grade girl. I recognized my jacket, but in seventh grade I couldn't have confronted a Twinkie, let alone a full-grown ninth grader. How had I ever considered myself gang-worthy?

When my mother remarried and we moved to 17th Avenue, my allegiance shifted from Big Chief to Weingarten's. It was closer now. Also, I had gone from taking myself seriously to being seriously prissy in record time, and I would have put my hair back in pigtails before I sat on the floor by a magazine stand ever again.

But the main attraction at Weingarten's was the bag boys. Now there's a dying occupation (no girls need apply – we were too delicate). These days you hope your checker doesn't put the watermelon on top of the bread, but since the bag boy is usually you, it can be avoided. At Weingarten's in the early '60s, a crew cut kid in a white shirt and black bow tie took great care, and even carried your bags to the car. In the eyes of a 14-year-old girl, they were men, especially Terry. He was too old for me, according to my mother, but he was once in love with my friend Rhonda, so I was acquainted with him because of his interest in her.

168. Terry Covington, U.S.M.C photo.

Weingarten's also piqued my interest because actual *thoughts* now lurked behind my thoughtful expression. My introduction to social injustice came courtesy of Weingarten's. When racial tensions heated up and there were sit-ins around the country, management at corporate headquarters in Houston decided to have the stools removed from all Weingarten's lunch counters. There. No Negroes could sit down. And neither could anyone else.

After his career at Weingarten's, Terry became a lifeguard at the TC swimming pool, and then head lifeguard when he was home from college during the summer. I probably never would have thought of the Red Coats again except for him.

By the time I was in high school and he was in college, he was over Rhonda, and he noticed I was alive. In response to a dare I plunged off the high diving board, screaming all the way down (12 whole feet). Then I didn't get out of the diving lane fast enough, a major swimming pool infraction. Terry blew his whistle like a crazy man.

I climbed out of the pool and said I was sorry, so from high on his wooden perch he peered down the front of my bathing suit and asked me for a date. Although he didn't seem as cute with zinc oxide on his nose, I accepted (my mother had relaxed her

169. Lunch counter with stools removed.
Where will the "ladies who lunch" sit now?

age-gap rules by then). Terry took me to see *West Side Story*.

Afterwards, sitting at the Terrace drive-in eating a tiny burger, I casually wondered if TC ever had a gang called the Red Coats. Terry had the answer. *Yes. It did.* He knew, because he was present at their demise.

And this is the tale he told me.

The leader of the Red Coats (I'll call him Red) and the leader of the Weingarten's bag boys (Bow-tie) fell in love with the same girl (according to Terry – all according to Terry).

So being in love with the same girl – classic – caused friction between Red and Bow-tie. Apparently, the girl had no say in settling the matter. It was up to the guys to work it out. Red called up Bow-tie at Weingarten's and threatened him. If Bow-tie didn't cease his pursuit of the young lady, there would be consequences. Bow-tie took the call in the back of the store within earshot of the other bag boys. Naturally, because of the audience, Bow-tie had to respond with bravado, something along the lines of:

Oh yeah? sneered Bow-tie. A pause. *Naw. We have to mop the floors and clean the toilets first. Me and my guys will meet you in the parking lot. At 11:30. Unless you're chicken. You're not chicken, are you?*

170. Grocery store bag boys.
Obviously looking for trouble.

So the rumble was on. Terry said the bag boys all huffed and puffed and agreed something had to be done, but secretly they were less than thrilled to be part of "my guys" in this context. Still, no one could admit to being chicken.

At 11:30 the bag boys filed out of the store, one by one, leaving a night watchman inside to lock up and possibly call an ambulance.

The Red Coats emerged from the shadows at the edge of the parking lot, red jackets looking black in the dim light, sinister with their defiant ducktails and turned up collars.

The bag boys lined up in V-formation, Bow-tie at the tip of the V, ready to meet their destiny, white shirts gleaming, bow ties straight and proud, crew cuts stiff in the breeze from Galveston Bay.

"I myself," Terry said with a grin, "found a place as far back as I could and still stay in the parking lot. I had my car keys in my hand."

I was thrilled. "As a weapon?"

"Heck, no! For a quick get-away."

On that night, the Red Coats took a step forward. The bag boys took a step forward. The neon sign flickered off and on.

Weingarten's - Better Food for Less.

Weingarten's - Better Food for Less.

For a full minute nothing happened except a staring contest.

Weingarten's - Better Food for Less.

The tension mounted. "This is crap," Bow-tie muttered.

"Yeah," said Red.

Bow-tie took two long strides and landed a punch square on Red's jaw. Just as the night watchman switched off the Weingarten's sign, Red's lights went out, too. He lay as still as an oil slick. Could it be over? Another Red Coat stepped forward, arms up, palms forward, making it clear he wasn't interested in retaliation.

He knelt by Red, who was trying to stand, but his knees wobbled. His pals carried him away. The Red Coats skulked back into the shadows and were gone. To the relief of the bag boys and probably the gang, too, it was over. No one else had to provide proof of non-chickeness.

"So the good guy got the girl?" I inquired.

Terry had no idea what happened to the girl, and I refrained from asking what the point was, if it wasn't about the girl. One more entry in the ledger of reasons I would never understand boys. Terry finished the story by saying Red was so humiliated he moved to Baytown and was never seen in Texas City again.

Was it a fairy tale or a Terry tale? Was it a tale full of sound and fury, just a boy trying to impress a girl? Or was it true? Even as Terry told the story I munched my tiny burger and tried to sort it out, but I didn't know the truth then, and I don't know it now. Somehow, though, the story makes perfect sense for Texas City as it was then.

I liked Big Chief, I liked Weingarten's, and I liked Terry, and in the context of the times, I choose to believe in a dark parking lot in the '60s, the Weingarten's bag boys broke the back of the Texas City Red Coats. And everyone lived happily ever after.

CHAPTER SEVENTEEN

My Favorite and Other Love Stories

171. Diane Howell and Joe Gillespie, side by side in the yearbook, and together still.

Only a fool would write about love. And so, boldly, I will.

172. Tommy Murphy and Kathleen Kelly

The strobe of young love pulsed through the halls of Texas City High School and led to matrimony many times, yet when I made up my mind to write through this rich material, I discovered that beyond gossip and speculation, I know nothing except the titles.

At the top of a chronology would be *The Story of Joe and Diane*,

173. Jean Haack and Gene King on their wedding day.

The Story of *Tommy and Kathleen, The Story of Virginia and Felix*. Joe and Diane's story continues, as does Tommy and Kathleen's.

Virginia and Felix ended long ago. The story I know best would be called *Gene and Jeannie*. Still together, still happy.

Infatuation should be enjoyed or endured and never taken seriously. It feels awful except when it feels wonderful. This kind of catastrophe can change and become love, and that's lucky. You have something then. There's a quote heard frequently from Hollywood starlets who mistake cliché for wisdom. *I still love him, but I'm not in love with him anymore.* They move on to another infatuation and never know they walked away from the best part of love.

174. Tommy Drake and Jeanie Vandaveer

Dolores and Jimmy didn't last, but I remember them together, tall and beautiful, both of them, way beyond the bloom of youth which belongs to us all for a short time. I've been told about Ray and Jeanie, on again/off again, then on again and off for good. Much later came *The Jeanie and Tommy Story.* Sandy McWhirter and *Dennis* Thompson over time became Sandy and *Eddie* Thompson. One less last name. Elegant Julia Hendrick married adorable Charlie Hobbs, but Julia and Charlie didn't last. That's all I know about it.

But my favorite love story of a Texas City girl, a story I know from beginning to end, might be called *The Painter, the Pilot, and the Texas Boy.* The Painter would be my mother's sister Dorothy Benskin, TC Central High (later TC High School), Class of 1942. Never fond of *Dorothy*, she would be called *Duffy* as a child, *Jinx* as a grown-up.

175. Central High newspaper, The Nautilus, December 1941.

Her talent for art surfaced early. She loved to draw, and she was good at it. Here's the cover of the Central High newspaper from December 1941. You'll recognize the school in the background if you grew up in TC. You can't see the tiny writing down by the cover girl's bag, but it identifies the cover artist as Dorothy Benskin.

Dorothy/Jinx loved two men in her life, and she dared to love them both forever. "Why should it not be so?" she told me. "We commit to one person and consign the others to memory, but the heart is a big place and true love lasts." So spoke Jinx, long ago.

Just out of her teens, Jinx fell in love with John, a Texas boy from San Saba County. She met him at a church social, and she described him as the handsomest man she ever saw. His passionate reaction to her perceived capriciousness makes me believe he loved her as she loved him.

Came World War II, and John was to travel through Houston on his way overseas, just to spend a few final hours with Jinx, who was living and working there. He might be killed, but for sure he would be gone for a long time. He

176. John Dean

couldn't tell her when he would be there, not the hour, anyway, but the day, at least. He would call, and they would arrange to meet.

She waited by the phone at work, but she had a task that would take her away from her desk, just for moments. When she could put it off no longer, she left, glancing anxiously at the clock. When she returned, she noted she had been gone for seven minutes. He couldn't have called. But he

177. Jinx, shortly after she was married.

had. The little yellow message lay on her desk like a rebuke. *Caller: Lt Dean. Time: When you were out.*

She waited the rest of the day for a call that had come and gone forever. The next word from John came in a letter. He had asked her

178. Lt. Lynn Steiner, 1946, U.S. Army Air Corps.

to wait, and she hadn't. How could he trust her for an entire war? Deeply angry, he wrote words so harsh she couldn't repeat them. He left for Europe and married an English girl within two months. Dusty, her name was.

"*Dusty* Dean," Jinx said. "I was supposed to be *Duffy* Dean." She used her old nickname, the one my mother gave her as a child.

So she moved to Florida with my mother and their cousins, where she met Lt Mahlon (Lynn) Steiner, a promising young pilot.

When Lynn proposed marriage, Jinx accepted him.

He loved flying airplanes, and he decided to stay in the military. When he was sent to Colorado for additional training, Jinx went home to Texas and prepared to be married. She received the attentions of a bride-to-be, showers, gifts, and fare-thee-wells as she boarded a bus headed west. They would become man and wife in a military chapel.

Lynn arranged for a hotel, and Jinx walked there from the bus station. He couldn't come by until after his training session, and when he did, she threw herself into his arms. He embraced her tentatively, holding back. He had something to say.

"I can't go through with it. I can't marry you. Forgive me."

Did Jinx's heart break? Did she cry or scream? No. She wondered how she would explain this to her mother. *What will mother think* informs a woman's life, intentions, behavior, forever.

"OK, then," was all she said to Lynn. "I'll be on a bus back to Texas as soon as I can."

He left, and she hardly noticed. She was already rehearsing her explanations. She would have time to think on the bus, so she thumbed through the telephone book, looking for *Greyhound*. Tires screeched in the parking lot and a car door slammed. She put down the phone at the pounding on the stairs. The door to her dingy room slammed opened, and there stood Lynn.

"I don't see how I could NOT marry a girl who could take that kind of news with such *sangfroid*," he said.

She waited until later to look up *sangfroid*, and she never told him his loss was way down on her list of problems that day. All she could think of was the humiliation of going home with her veil between her legs.

Jinx came to adore Lynn, bore his children, embraced his church, lived his life, and wanted him to love her as intensely as she loved him. Yet the memory of John rested quietly, just in case a change in circumstance might make it blossom again, as young romances do, and often, because of death or divorce, sometimes just because.

Twenty minutes after the wedding, she became pregnant. Lynn, a good Catholic, would hear of no birth control except the ones that didn't work – rhythm and abstinence, abstinence being particularly ineffective in the case of young newlyweds.

Jinx didn't recognize the early signs of pregnancy, then one morning she got all soaped up in the shower and suddenly felt faint. She whispered *Lynn*, and he heard her from two rooms away with the radio on. When a loved one calls for help, you hear it.

He got to the shower, and she was slippery as a Texas con artist, naked as an egg, and swooning. Lynn, his khaki uniform turning dark brown and soggy, clutched at her, got enough grip to keep her from getting hurt, then dragged her onto the bathroom rug as she came around.

"What the hell, Lynn?" she said. "I weigh 110 pounds. Can't you just pick me up?"

They stared at each other, a soapy naked pregnant lady and a wet military officer with his dignity askew. She laughed. He didn't.

179. My glamorous Aunt Jinx, 1954.

So they had their first child, my cousin Mary Lynne. Jinx got pregnant again at once, but when he was born, baby Tony was sick. Lynn was soon on his way to his new assignment in occupied Japan. Jinx stayed behind with the children, but not for long. She left the baby boy in the care of her mother-in-law, and joined her husband with their daughter in tow.

Your man *über alles* was the order of things, plus Jinx thought Lynn was playing around. Why did she think that, I once asked? He was a man, she said, alone and far away. He was handsome and charming. If he wasn't playing around already, he soon would be.

Long after all the principals were dead, I found a letter from Jinx's mother-in-law to my grandmother (Jinx's mother) dated December 12, 1949, from Los Angeles.

I have sad news for you. Little Tony passed away last night at the Children's Hospital at 8:30.

It goes into detail, and from that letter I learned the baby wasn't

180. Aunt Jinx's portraits of me (age 16), my mother (age 40), and my sister Tish (age 10).

sick. He was hydrocephalic, almost certain to die in infancy. When he did, neither Jinx nor Lynn returned from Japan. In 1949 it would have taken days, maybe weeks.

As for John, Jinx's first love, in 1946 my mother sent Jinx an article from a San Saba newspaper with a picture of John Dean. He had survived the war and been awarded the Distinguished Flying Cross. Beyond that, Jinx knew nothing of him for the next 30 years, yet, in spite of her love for Lynn, she thought of John often.

My aunt had a comfortable life, but restlessness defined her. She wanted the elusive *more* that haunted generations of women, even though being the wife of a military officer was supposed to be enough. She revisited her gift for drawing and painting. Her work gave her some of the satisfaction she sought, and some recognition and success as a portrait painter. She painted almost everyone in the Benskin family, and all of us were thrilled to be given gifts of her work on special occasions.

To be a better military wife, she went to charm school and learned the tricks of modeling and makeup. She learned to entertain graciously, as was expected of her.

Jinx and her family lived in far-away places, and when they came through Texas City, fresh from being stationed in Hawaii, all colorful muumuus and suntans, I glimpsed a life entirely unknown to me. My aunt, whom I adored, lived a glamorous life,

181. Jinx worshipping Lynn.

she had style and taste. Her sons were darling, her daughter was gorgeous.

Jinx had wit, too, and a world view I found entertaining and astonishing. I have a mental image of her perched on a bar stool at a beach dive in Galveston, holding court, wielding a wine glass. "Benskins either go crazy or become artists," she pronounced. "And some become crazy artists. Or must you be crazy to be an artist?"

All the while, Lynn remained aloof, never giving Jinx the attention and affection she craved. Once when they were living in New Mexico, Lynn went out on a training flight, and as she prepared dinner, she casually hoped he would crash.

182. Jinx's daughter Mary Lynn, in her stewardess days.

He came home safe, and she didn't truly want him to crash except in that secret way we dream of a simpler life, a life without *the other*. In that moment, though, Jinx understood the yearning to be close to Lynn, so long unfulfilled, was gone for good. Did he sense the sea change? Know his decades-long upper hand had vanished? Jinx said he didn't. Nothing changed for him.

Years passed. I was 21 years old, single, and living in Wiesbaden, Germany, working for the U.S. Air Force. My mother made plans to visit, and Jinx decided to come with her.

My friend and classmate Gloria Moseley had joined me on this adventure, had met a good-looking young GI from Texas, and they decided to marry (and are still married).

As it happened, the visit of my mother and my aunt coincided with Gloria's matrimonial plans, which was perfect. She knew my mother well, and it felt good to have someone from home at the wedding. After the ceremony in Switzerland, on the way back to Wiesbaden, Jinx dropped a bomb.

183. Gloria's wedding in Basel, Switzerland. My mother, Randy Rodriguez (the best man), me (maid of honor), Gloria, Tex Buehring (the groom), and Aunt Jinx.

She didn't come to see me. She came to see John. Texas ties never die, so someone told my grandmother, who told my mother, who told Jinx, that John lived in nearby Frankfurt with his wife. Jinx wrote him; he wrote back. I was shocked. I had never heard his name. She told me about him then, the war, the missed phone call, the acid letter, his hasty marriage, the fractures in her own union.

So John showed up, still tall and good-looking, and with his own driver. He and Jinx went off for the afternoon. I don't know what he told his wife, but this happened several times. Jinx swore all they did was talk. I believed her, because I couldn't imagine anything else. After all, they were in their early 40s, well past all that, right?

Mostly I believed her because John's leg was in a cast from ankle to groin, and he was on crutches. That's why he needed a driver. Two months before his reunion with Jinx, he fell off a camel in Egypt and broke his leg in two places (no one could make this stuff up).

Meanwhile, retired from the military and working for Raytheon in

184. Jinx and Virgil.

Newport News, Lynn eagerly awaited Jinx's return, not knowing he had a shock coming. On her first day back in Virginia she asked him for a divorce.

Her daughter Mary Lynne was by then on her own, so Jinx packed up her teenage boys and went home to Texas. Did she assume John would leave Dusty? That she and John would live happily ever after? He did not; they did not. Were promises made? She never clarified this detail. If so, they weren't kept, at least not by John.

As for Lynn, he realized at last Jinx was the great passion of his life, and he wanted her back, right now, and badly. In a fairly short time, Jinx understood she had made a mistake.

185. Lt Col Lynn Steiner's interment at Arlington National Cemetery.

She missed her comfortable life, and she missed Lynn. She was used to him. She called to tell him she was coming back, but he had big news, and he spoke first. He had met a nice lady named Sarah, and they were to be wed. That's love for you.

My aunt was lonely and married phlegmatic Virgil, but left him in a few years. The Centers for Disease Control in Atlanta, my employer at the time, sent me to Austin on business, so afterwards I rented a car

186. Pat Pryor and Gail Sanders

and drove to the coast to visit my mother and Jinx. Sitting in Jinx's living room, drinking wine, laughing it up, I asked when her divorce would be final. She said never. She had no reason to divorce Virgil, and if he died, she would inherit certain benefits. He was OK with the arrangement, since he had no other family. Virgil died that night. It's likely he died while we were discussing the matter.

Lynn and Sarah were married longer than Lynn and Jinx. Jinx died first, and then Lynn. I met Sarah at his interment in Arlington National Cemetery, and a few years later I ran into her in Williamsburg. My husband and I were visiting friends, who invited several others to join us at a restaurant. One of them was Sarah. What are the odds? She seemed uncomfortable. Perhaps she sensed that to me, she was an imposter. My aunt was Lynn's true wife and true widow, and that would never change in my world view.

As for John, I imagine he's dead by now. Dusty, his wife, died before Jinx. but John still didn't seek out the arms of my aunt, even though she was single, too, having just buried Virgil. Maybe too much water goes under too many bridges after a while, either in love or infatuation.

So here's to the love stories of the TCHS Class of '64, the ones that lasted, like Gail and Pat, and the ones that didn't, sad or radiant, enduring or short, productive or a waste, sometimes as byzantine as Jinx's saga. Whatever the outcome, all I can tell you is the titles, and anyway, only a fool would write about love.

This last picture comes from the 1942 Central High Yearbook. My Aunt Jinx can be seen, top row, second from left, before either of her love stories, before she was old, before time took its toll.

But I remember her story, and I can tell it. And after all, everyone loves a love story.

187. Texas City Central High Yearbook, 1942.
Photo courtesy of Al Mitchell.

CHAPTER EIGHTEEN

First Love

I attended a high school reunion when I was 19 years old. I spent the evening thinking about love and hoping to meet Paula Prentiss. By the end of the event, I learned there's love, there's infatuation, and then there's first love, a thing apart. And Paula wasn't coming.

It wasn't my own reunion, of course, but the tenth reunion of Larry, my date, a 29-year-old astronaut candidate who worked for NASA and drove a red Porsche. He spent his work days figuring out how to keep people from burning up in space. I spent my work days in the NASA awards office, wondering what Larry saw in me. I was infatuated and impressed.

188. Paula Prentiss, 1965.

Larry graduated from high school in Houston, and we had been dating for six months when he took me to his reunion. The Lamar High School Class of 1956 included Paula Ragusa, who went to Hollywood and turned into Paula Prentiss. No one knew if she would come to the reunion, and when she didn't, Larry suggested her lack of interest might have something to do with being called Paula the Bean Pole for three years in high school. She had the last laugh, that's for sure.

I felt out of my depth with so many grown-ups, so I smiled and said little. Larry introduced me to his best friend from the old days, and I curtsied but kept my resolve not to giggle or otherwise reveal myself to be so young. In a few weeks I would turn 20, and Larry said he would be relieved not to be smitten with a teenager.

I resisted the urge to scream when the friend shook my hand and began to squeeze so hard I thought my fingers would scream for me. I looked at him, but he was looking past me, smiling into the distance. He raised the other hand in a combination wave and salute. He didn't realize he had my hand in a death grip, because I didn't exist for him. He had seen someone across the room. He dropped my hand and walked away. I asked Larry what that was about.

"His high school sweetheart. First love. That's her in the blue dress. Still beautiful, I see."

"His heart still throbs; my hand still throbs." I shook my wrist, and he laughed. I made him laugh. Maybe that's why he liked me. Maybe he'd forgiven me for thinking his Porsche was a Volkswagen on our first date.

"She burned him pretty bad. It was rocky at worst, intense at best."

"Ten years later, and he loved her best?"

"Best? No. Not *best*. He loved her *first*. There's love, and there's first love. You only feel like that once."

The remark rang true; I filed it away for future evaluation.

****

Forget the past? Live in the present? If you like, but I love to visit the past, and to re-experience the good things about growing up in a small town in a gentler time. The past and present are not mutually exclusive, and we learn from the past. Experience smartens us up as much as formal schooling.

Writing about love once may be too often, but I can't help it. When I re-visit junior year, I think about love. When school started it seemed everyone at TCHS was in love except me. My sailor boyfriend was gone, and the only thing I loved was the fun of dating, especially because while some girls liked "bad boys," I liked nice guys.

189. Janice Biery

I dated Jerry, the brother of a classmate, a little older, and smart. I liked him and respected him, and I remember him fondly. I dated Terry the lifeguard, who had the keys to the swimming pool, and we sometimes sneaked in after hours with two or three other couples. No one suggested we go skinny dipping. The boys were gentlemen, and the girls were ladies.

At the tail end of 10th grade there was Vic the TCHS track star. His pal Eddie dated Janice. Victor and Eddie crowned us "Track Queens" (no snickering, please), so we dressed up and handed out medals at track meets. We didn't get our picture in the yearbook, which we both thought was too bad. Vic was unhappy because I wouldn't promise to date only him. He called to give me one last chance. I refused. He stopped calling.

I was having a great time, but I wondered what it would be like to be in love like Karen and Mike. I observed a harmony between them, a calmness under the excitement. I'm happy they stayed together; it would have disappointed me if they hadn't. I observed other couples, too, who claimed to be in love. The first time I heard the F word out loud was from a girl, screaming in the face of a boy she was supposed to love. I didn't think they would last; they didn't.

Then I did fall in love.

In small towns, you don't meet someone as it's frequently put. You already know them if they're even close to your age. Everyone has a connection. You know the brother of that one, the cousin of this one. I knew Charlie because he was Gene's best friend, and I knew Gene from the time I was in sixth or seventh grade.

190. Mike Hemingway and Karen Brown

Funny, how you remember one morning among hundreds of others. One morning I sat in my friend Carolyn's car in the parking lot at TCHS. There were spaces along the curb, even late in the morning, because no one could parallel park. Maybe that's why I watched with interest as Charlie pulled up and skillfully parked his 1953 Chevy ragtop. The top was down, and he and his friends got out of the car and manually tugged it back in place. I thought Charlie was attractive, but serious and dignified. Not my type at all, even though his parallel parking technique impressed me.

We had a class together and had spoken a few times, but I was surprised when he called and asked me for a date. I said no, I was busy, but try again some time. He did, and I said yes.

We went to the Thespian play with Gene and Jeannie -- compatible then and for a lifetime. To illustrate the fickleness of memory, I recall Charlie parking the Chevy as though it happened last week. The 1963 yearbook indicates the play was *Guys and Dolls*, and even though a few years later I would perform in that play myself, I had no recollection of seeing it in high school. Memory has a mind of its own.

191. Charles Edward Elfstrom

Soon Charlie and I were going out every weekend, and soon we were in love, but I disliked his car. The submarine races on the dike attracted couples, and it was the duty of those without dates to honk and harass the young lovers, but I couldn't figure out how they recognized us in the dark from 30 yards away. They called out to Charlie and me by name. I hated that, but I envied their eyesight, and I said so.

Charlie laughed. "They don't recognize us. They know the car. Who else has a '53 Chevy convertible?" Welcome to Our Town.

What was it like, then, to be in love? Although the car was unique (I was relieved when it was traded), our romance probably wasn't, but it was real, and it makes me smile to think we truly believed no one else ever felt like that. Judging by the burgeoning population of the world, it should have been evident, even to high school kids, that many people did feel like that, and took it one step further than we ever dared.

If there was anything unusual about Charlie and me, it was that we knew we weren't a good match. We wanted different things from life. I dealt with it by being angry; he dealt with it by denial, but perhaps that knowledge gave our relationship a poignancy it would not otherwise have had.

192. 1953 Chevy convertible, about like Charlie's.

I wonder about high school sweethearts who marry and stay married. Do they sometimes recapture the magical feeling of first love? Do they wonder who they might have loved but never knew? Do I wonder what my life would have been like if I'd made different choices? The answer is three times yes. We have to choose, and we do, mostly without regret, but in our minds we all stroll down the road not taken now and then.

****

Most men would rather drink an acid martini with exploding olives than share the smallest inner thought, but writers are an exception. Tom the Writer, a friend in my Atlanta days, had much to say about everything. We were in a creative writing class, and toward the end of the term, a group of us formed the habit of meeting for drinks afterward.

We sipped our wine and pondered our next assignment, which was 2,000 words on the subject of first love. We agreed it was a cliché, usually a high school event 30 years ago for most of the group. But Tom sparked a conversation. He posited that the experience of first love for girls is just a trial run, while it's devastating for boys. It leaves them gob-smacked, said Writer Tom from Tennessee.

"Girls expect it, hope for it. Guys don't. We know there are girls around, but some time in high school, maybe junior year, they aren't girls any more. They're radiant young women. You cannot imagine the effect that can have on a 17-year-old boy. Yup. Gob-smacked."

I went home to think about that. I couldn't imagine being a boy from the TCHS class of '64, any more than I could imagine being a duck, but then again, I knew ducks quacked and lived in marshes, and I knew the boys made a lot of noise, and I knew their habitat.

I knew the times, the Saturday night places. The boys pooled their quarters for gas money to drive up and down Sixth Street, or sneak a trunkload of pals into the Tradewinds drive-in movie, where the concession had the best French fries in town.

They went to the Terrace drive-in restaurant where protocol dictated the approach. They thought they were doing something daring and wild, yet everyone obeyed the exact rules for "dragging" the Terrace. Enter on the left side, drive around and across the front to see and be seen, then exit to the right back to the highway. Only then did you pull into a spot at the back. One night a sophomore halfway through "the drag" hit a support post on the awning, and the awning collapsed onto the cars. Biggest thing to happen all year.

193. Mary Nell Hunt, a beautiful young *woman*.

But was Tom right? Did female creatures the boys only tolerated become interesting, even distracting, almost overnight? Were the halls a river of beautiful, poised, smiling young women, all bright eyes and tight skirts? And OMG, they had breasts!

I spent a little time with my yearbooks open so I could compare how people looked year to year. Picture to picture like magic, the girls turned into women. As for the boys, if it wasn't for the suits and ties, they would all look like fifth-graders. Good-looking, yes, but not like grown men. Not yet.

It must have been crazy-making when one day a girl came into class late and smiled. The boy felt weird. He thought, *What the hell?* The girl slid into the desk in front of him, and he couldn't look at anything except her long, shiny hair. He had no idea what just happened, but he had to do something about it. He called her up and asked her out.

In one month and six dates the boy was hopelessly in love. After that, he couldn't breathe unless he knew where she was, what she was doing, and when he could see her again. And OMG, could he bed her?

194. Mary Morgan, definitely a lovely young *woman*.

And what was the girl thinking? Something along the lines of *OK, here it is. Good. Let's see what happens. Go all the way? Never. Well. Maybe.*

But probably not.

Because the girls of the class of '64 were *The Last Convertible, The Last of the Mohicans, and the Last Picture Show* all rolled into bows, headbands, and big, innocent eyes, sexy without baring all, alluring because they were unattainable. Not that they couldn't be seduced, but it was on their own terms, with their own conditions, and defined by their relationships. In a few years the women's movement would change the rules, some for better,

195. *Boyishly* handsome Louis Sholmire.

some for worse. For all the freedom and new paths open to women, the girls of the class of '64 had one freedom that stands out as it drib-

196. *Boyishly* handsome Al Van Amberg.

bles away. They had the freedom to say *no* emphatically, and without apology or explanation.

Before all the rules changed, the girls didn't think much about football or grades. They thought of the inevitable moment when they would fall in love for the first time. They dreamed about it and imagined it, even practiced it in junior high. They knew it was coming, and when it did, it was the right and proper thing. They took it in stride. They were not gobsmacked.

No wonder the boys were stunned at the spectacular transformations as little girls grew up, lovely and comfortable with themselves, most of the angst left behind in junior high. The boys would catch up and catch on, and then girls took it all harder, but high school love? Yes, Writer Tom had it right. First love, at least in those days, was harder on boys.

Now that we have the internet, most wonderful invention in the world, I know how so many stories ended, and what a satisfying thing that is to a storyteller.

Paula Prentiss, who didn't come to the reunion of the Lamar High Class of 1956, turned out to be one of the rarest of Hollywood stars. She married Richard Benjamin, her college sweetheart, in 1958, and they're married still.

Larry from long ago never became an astronaut. He got cut in the next round. He did get his PhD and held several patents, including one for a method to weigh astronauts in zero gravity. He married, and he died of leukemia in 2012.

But just as Tom was right about first love being hard on boys, Larry was right about first love being unique. By definition it only happens once, and you don't forget it. Falling in love never feels the same as it does when you're 17 years old. What happens later is better, finer, more lasting, but never the giddy same.

In the spring of sophomore year, I dated John for a short time. I wasn't in love, but I'll never forget him because he was the first young man to send me roses. I also remember the first time I had lasagna, at Pino's near University of Houston, and even though I've eaten that delicious dish many times since, I'll never forget that first time at Pino's.

Charlie found his lasting love, and so did I. Both memory and feelings are abstract, and it's twice abstract to remember a feeling. Long after it's over, everyone remembers how it felt to be in love for the first time. Unless it grew into something else, beyond infatuation or first love, you seldom loved your high school sweetheart *best*, but you did love them *first*.

And you always remember the first time for anything, be it roses, romance, breakfast on the Eiffel Tower, or lasagna. Or love.

CHAPTER NINETEEN

Here We Are, There Ain't No More

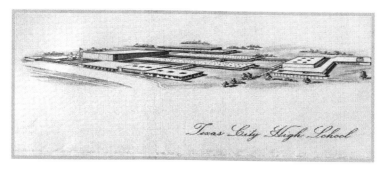

197. Standard TCHS Graduation Invitation.

History, unpredictable, relentless, and over-whelming, and like water, benign until an earthquake raises a tsunami of change, and you adapt or get swept away, shredded. The class of '64 would graduate into an unrecognizable world. And it's always been so. My aunts, of another generation, both made a similar observation comparing the '40s to the '60s, and it was this, simple but powerful as water: "Things are so different now."

The mid- and late-'60s shift in my head like a kaleidoscope, but I keep a permanent vision of the summer of 1963.

Bright, smooth water, reflecting silver, disturbed only by the wake of a boat and the rooster tail from a single ski. Turquoise sky, winsome girls in bathing suits, strong boys, quick and agile. Even the sound of the motor vanished into white noise, refusing to disturb the

198. Lloyd Lambert

tranquility of sky, water, and youth. We float through time on an unchanged surface, forever. Even the songs have a water theme. Surf City. Surfin' USA.

Lloyd's dad trusts him with a ski rig, and in the rosy hue of memory the boat is pink. Lloyd, Gene, Charlie, and sometimes Rusty, pick us up one by one, Sue, Jeannie, and me (Rusty never brings the same girl twice). They launch the boat on Dickenson Bayou, and I admire how careful they are, how conscientious of Mr. Lambert's trust. They are men already, grown-up and responsible in behavior if not appearance.

A short ride down the bayou to a place we called "the point," to unload the cooler, blankets and towels. We ski and picnic all afternoon, and when we're done we clean up after ourselves. We don't drink. We wear our life jackets. On the water, we keep the high-jinks to a minimum, though we are lively kids. Rusty rides his skis over a grassy outcropping and right back onto the bayou, and he yells boo rah like the Navy SEAL he will one day be. Charlie

199. Rusty Girardin

skies way too close to a tied-up barge, trails his hand along the top of it, and scares the dickens out of me. Long-legged Gene flies above the wake and makes it look easy. The girls ski well enough, but none of us has the athleticism of the boys.

How could we have seen the swell of social change under such calm water?

This was my season of magical thinking. Nothing would change. I wouldn't let it. My personal challenges were behind me. I had managed life at Danforth and groped my way through Blocker Junior High. I accepted the abandonment of my father and

200. Sue Anderson

experienced Hurricane Carla. Early in 1963 my mother almost died at Danforth Hospital of pernicious anemia, and on the way from Baytown to help me cope, my stepfather's sister met a truck head-on out on Highway 45. She was killed, and my mother's post-surgery care fell to me, until my stepfather could arrange to be relieved from his job on the river. I missed a week of school, and it was hard to make it up.

The Cuban Missile Crisis elevated fears of nuclear holocaust, but it didn't happen, because our young, handsome, capable president would see that it didn't. No one had ever heard of Vietnam, and we couldn't have found it on a map if we had. So nothing bad could happen, and senior year would begin but never end.

I looked forward to August, when I would go somewhere at last. My only formal extracurricular activity was Junior Achievement, and my company was Mijet II. We should have been disqualified because of the silly name. We spelled it funny for no reason, pronounced it *midget,* and the *II* was because the previous year we had been just *Mijet.*

However, I guess our experience paid off, because Mijet II won first runner-up for best-managed Junior Achievement companies among 674 entries. The prize was three all-expense paid trips to the National J.A. Conference at the University of Indiana in Bloomington. I was selected to go, along with Gloria from TCHS and Marie from LaMarque High School.

City, Texas, Friday, August 16, 1963   Daily 5c

201. Gloria Moseley, Marie Mickie (?), and me. The caption in the TC Sun was "All Dressed up and Someplace to Go."

We flew to New Orleans, a first for all of us, and we joined a group of Achievers from Louisiana. From there we went by train to Indiana, picking up another group in Birmingham, and I got my first inkling of troubling times. The Birmingham police had set dogs and high-velocity fire hoses on its black citizens that spring, and the Birmingham group oozed ill-will, no doubt a reflection of their parents. There were black people on the train, and the Birmingham kids said things about what would happen if any of *them* dared enter our train car, sit at our table in the dining area, or speak to any of the white girls.

It may have been a beautiful summer on Dickenson Bayou, but 1963 was a wicked summer in Alabama. When school started in September TCHS would enroll black students for the first time, but I couldn't picture that kind of hate on the faces of my friends.

Once we arrived on the Indiana campus, I was billeted in a boy's dorm which was empty for the summer. The organizers, hoping to broaden our horizons, assigned everyone a roommate from a different part of the country, and mine came from Buffalo, New York. When I asked her about the white porcelain fixtures on the wall in the bathroom, she laughed out loud.

"Urinals, dummy. That's where the boys piss." She rummaged in her suitcase. "Where's my sax. I can't find my sax."

Well, how was I to know? I'd never been in a men's room, let alone heard a girl say that word. And she couldn't fine her *sax*? Had she lost her saxophone? Her *sex*? What?

Miss Buffalo waved a small white ball in her hand. "Here they are! My sax!"

"Oh," I said. "Your *socks*."

I contemplated my broadening horizons. I'd heard of urinals and now I'd seen them, and some girls said *piss* right out loud. And maybe I was a dummy, but at least I could pronounce the word *socks*.

I don't remember one thing about our organized J.A. learning sessions, but I remember someone blew a toilet off the wall with a cherry bomb. In the talent contest, a kid played a moving violin solo, but a kid doing stand-up comedy won by a show of applause, proving high school kids preferred comedy to the violin. I ran into Jimmy Kickbusch from Blocker (the boy Rhonda tried to steal from me). His family moved back east before high school, but there he was in a cafeteria line in Indiana, so I learned it truly is a small world.

The week flew by, and I felt astonishment at how quickly the hateful atmosphere resurfaced when we got back on the train for home. It stayed with us until we got to Birmingham.

Gloria was the best thing about the Indiana trip. I knew her from school and from Junior Achievement, and I admired her easy-going temperament and her bravery when her brother Dwayne was killed in a traffic accident up on Bay Street. After the trip we became better

202. Sherry Longshore

friends, and post-high school we shared an apartment in Houston for three years and many other great adventures.

When school started in the fall, I was a sophisticated senior. After all, I had been all the way to Indiana! I had been on a jet airplane. I lived in an amazing world of touch tone phones and zip codes. Soon there would be bubble wrap! Yes, the world was changing, alright. The end of the Studebaker would be followed in the spring by the car of the decade, the Ford Mustang. All other troublesome rumblings would pass away because time had stopped for me.

I loved Texas City High. Loved the well-lit hallways, polite students, and no-nonsense teachers. Whenever lining up was the order of the day, the unlucky alphabet placed me by Sherry and Mary Lynne (Long, Longshore, Lopez), and standing by these beauties, I imagined myself as a potato with a pony tail (oh, the insecurities of teenage girls). But they were both nice, and I got used to it.

I ignored the misgivings engendered by the Birmingham kids, and not long after the J.A. trip, I watched TV, enraptured, as Martin Luther King delivered his *I have a Dream speech*. It moved

203. Mary Lynne Lopez

me, made me think my school might be OK.

And it was. The black students invoked a few negative remarks, but in TC explosions that killed 600 people were cause for concern, and hurricanes that devastated the town. A few black kids was nothing to get upset about.

Now we could focus on important stuff, like football. Every Friday morning the sounds of the marching band bounced around the gym like the cheerleaders, and when *Dixie* became our *de facto* fight song, I never wondered if it was racist. The black students swayed and clapped with the rest of us, so maybe *Dixie* was (and is) just a catchy tune. What havoc political correctness reeks. As Freud famously said, sometimes a cigar is just a cigar.

The football game I remember best was at Baytown, and my boyfriend Charlie drove Linda and me to the stadium. Mid-game, with lots of time left and a few yards for a touchdown, one of the TC coaches (Coach Koonce?) decided to go for a field goal. Charlie and I thought the team should go for a touchdown, but Linda thought a field goal attempt was best. We won by three points (17 to 14), Linda was right, and winning a football game in high school meant more than it ever would again.

As for my academic life, by now I was used to my mother's spurious advice. Never wear your glasses (bad), don't get pregnant (excellent), and then came two sentences on the subject of my future. She suggested after graduation (as if there would be such thing), I ought to go to Hollywood and become a movie star. She thought that a viable plan. I did not. She shrugged, Butterfly style, at my lack of interest in becoming a star, and offered the last advice she ever gave me. It was practical, and I took it.

"Well, if you don't want to be a movie star, be sure you take typing."

Why wasn't I agitated about the future? Because in 1964 the preordained path of girls was to be a nurse, a teacher, or a secretary until you became a wife and mother. I love these traditional roles, and I also respect the exceptions, but at the time only 11.7 per cent of men in the U.S. had a college degree, and 6.8 per cent of women. College for girls meant the coveted MRS Degree. Yet I had a secret ambition. I wanted never to get married and to be totally independent, but I couldn't tell anyone. It wasn't what I was supposed to want.

On November 22, 1963, when things seemed safe, the earthquake occurred, and with it the rising tsunami of change. I've described the knock on the door of Mrs. Neyland's class, and the quiet way she told us of the events in Dallas.

There followed the bleak weekend of the funeral, and for a little while I wanted to hurry time, get past those dreadful days. When President Kennedy died, the '50s were done. Nothing would ever be the same, and even if our resilient hearts didn't break, our intuition told us something was gone, and it wasn't just our innocence. It was

the innocence of a whole nation, and the era of assassinations had begun. Bobby Kennedy would be next, in January of 1968, followed by Martin Luther King, Jr, in April of the same year. We were at least blessed not to know that.

And even as we mourned, the future was being written, and the past would be prologue. In January the Surgeon General concluded smoking caused cancer. In 2005 cancer would take my sister's life, and my mother's (both heavy smokers) in the same week. The Port Authority of New York and New Jersey released the designs for the

World Trade Center, which would be built and would fall, and would change the country even more than the Kennedy assassination.

After Christmas, things seemed marginally normal again, but in February Betty Friedan published a best-selling and controversial book, *The Feminine Mystique.* I read it, and I didn't know what to think, but whatever the problem *that had no name* was, my Aunt Jinx had it. The coming feminist movement? You could have told me people would one day surgically change their gender, and I wouldn't have believed any of it.

A huge irony occurred that spring. Not only was Mrs. Neyland's class the place we learned of the worst event of senior year, it was also the venue of the most hilarious. She decided we would benefit by reading *The King and I* out loud, and Fred would read the part of the king. Adorable Fred, who looked about as kingly as Charlie Brown, but he gamely read the lines, and at Mrs. Neyland's urging he put gusto into his work.

204. Fred Tooley, aka the King of Siam.

I don't believe I mentioned Mrs. Neyland's lisp, but she did have one. We snickered about it as teenagers will do, but she knew how to rule a classroom, and we respected her. Still, Fred was *Thread* for a whole year in English class.

He was reading the scene in which the King emphasizes to Anna that HE is KING, and SHE only a lowly school teacher, and her head should never be higher than his. To keep it that way, he had some instructions:

"When I *stand*, you *stand*. When I *sit*, you *sit*."

"Put some life into it, *Thread*," Mrs. Neyland encouraged.

So this is what he said: "When I stand, you stand!!" And then, with great emphasis and enthusiasm: "When I *shit*, you *shit!!*"

The class roared. We were stifling our amusement, as we always did, at Mrs. Neyland's lisp, but when Thread said that, it was over. The class roared. I'll never again see a human being turn that red. There ought to be a crayon called: Fred Red. He stood there wishing he was in Siam or dead, while his face became the reddest thing I ever saw, before or since.

Mrs. Neyland allowed us our laugh. She even laughed a bit herself, once she determined he didn't do it on purpose, but when she was ready, she whipped us in line again, but we didn't forget that scene from *The King and I.* I saw the play in Los Angeles 30 years later, and I laughed out loud at that line, the one Fred fumbled so spectacularly. I was the only one in the audience who did, and only I knew why.

****

The days slipped away, and my Aunt Jackie wanted to give me a graduation party, which terrified me. Would anyone come? March seemed way too soon, but Aunt Jackie said it was perfect. I wanted to

205. Aunt Jackie, looking very '60's on 21st Avenue.

go to Australia or be put in prison, anything to avoid this party which would be a failure. Instead, I agreed to the ordeal.

Did my aunt know she would guarantee my social season? I invited everyone I could think of to my graduation Coke party on 21st Avenue. Hard to believe I feel the need to clarify: In Texas *Coke* meant *soft drink* and not *cocaine* – yes, things have changed.

I got a great turn-out for the party due to the excitement of being among the first graduates to be so honored! Then I got invited to the parties of people who were invited to mine. Thank you, Aunt Jackie. My fabulous aunts. The one I love the most is always the one I'm thinking about.

John Medley

Quinton Bice

The same month Aunt Jackie gave me a Coke party, Robert McNamara told President Johnson that 40 per cent of South Vietnam was under control of the Viet Cong. I knew nothing of this, and didn't want to, but many of the young men of the class of '64 would know about it, and soon. Some, like John Medley and Quinton Bice, would put on a uniform and go to Southeast Asia, but they would not come back.

The tide that would wash away so much of what we knew and how we were raised was swelling, but we could remain untroubled for a little while. We could roll a few houses and stuff a few cars with shredded newspaper. Linda thought it was shameful to be seniors without ever skipping school, so we convinced Lana and Carolyn to do it. We went to Linda's house because both her parents worked, and we anticipated trouble when someone in the TCHS admin office called our homes. The office didn't bother. Not one of us had a "criminal record" at school, so they simply assumed we were sick. We were disappointed not to cause a kerfuffle, and surprised to learn going to school was more fun than skipping out.

Spring of 1964 and I still ignored the coming of graduation. It could never happen, because that would mean the end of high school. There was a huge private graduation party at the Elks Club, where the DJ played I *Wanna Hold Your Hand* by he Beatles about 20 million times. Charlie and I went to the dance at the Jack Tarr Hotel, to senior prom, and to Senior Night on the Town. And then, despite all my fantasies, graduation came. The most carefree days of my life were over.

Here we are, there ain't no more! Yay seniors '64.

Our class cheer, more prophetic than we imagined. The push of history works on all graduating classes, but not many grow up in

a world that changed irrevocably just as they were grown – the civil rights act, the women's movement, Vietnam, the drug culture. We weren't prepared, and yet, to our credit, most of us made the adjustments we had to make.

So the class of 1964? Are we happy and fulfilled? Is that a yes or no question? For most of us, it isn't that simple. For most of us, the answer is yes. And no. And maybe.

206. Graduation night, May 1964.

CHAPTER TWENTY

Well Done, Dennis Black

No man is an island,
Entire of itself.
Each is a piece of the continent,
A part of the main.
If a clod be washed away by the sea,
Europe is the less.
As well as if a promontory were.
As well as if a manor of thine own
Or of thine friend's were.
Each man's death diminishes me,
For I am involved in mankind.
Therefore, send not to know
For whom the bell tolls,
It tolls for thee.

For Whom the Bell Tolls
   a poem by John Donne

Dennis's death in 2016 was a tragedy for his sons and for Lisa, his wife, and for all those who loved him. I dislike the tendency to appropriate other people's grief, but I do claim a sense of loss, for as John Donne said, *each man's death diminishes me.* In March of 2016 that man was Dennis Black.

When Lisa gave us the sad news of Dennis' passing, she reminded us he popped into the world on Halloween of 1946 – probably scared the crap out of his mom and chuckled until he got whacked on the bottom by the doc. It's possible he arranged to move to Texas City so he could live where the school colors were orange and (Dennis) black. Can't you hear him making that claim just for fun? He almost died on April 1, but he died the day before. Perhaps witty Dennis thought April Fool's Day might be a good choice, but a little too predictable for the crazy smart boy-to-man that was our Dennis, a member of the Texas City High School Class of 1964.

Most of us know the last lines of John Donne's poem because of the novel by Ernest Hemmingway, *For Whom the Bell Tolls*, but each

**207. Dennis and me in the Danforth Elementary
School Choir. Photo courtesy of Al Mitchell.**

line resonates anew as we grow older. Dennis was known to me only a little growing up, but he lived in my neighborhood. He hung out at the Big Chief grocery store, sat on the floor and read comic books, as I did. He was in the choir at Danforth Elementary School, same as me, sporting a big green bow tied up like something weirdly Irish. He was woven into the fabric of that life, part of the continent, a piece of the main that was Texas City in the '50s and '60s.

Even as we walked the same playgrounds as children and knew the stories of our town's disaster, we lived under the threat of hurricanes locally and nuclear war globally. We passed in the halls of Blocker Junior High and TCHS, and took the short route on the Stingaree football field on graduation night. We went out into the world, and our paths ceased to cross for almost half a century, and then by some grace I can't explain, we walked together again.

I became aware of Dennis' goofy but highly intelligent wit from his offerings on Facebook, particularly regarding his wife, Lisa. His love for her showed every time he used her name, and Lisa was full of cheeky comebacks. I had a chance to speak to them briefly at our 50th reunion. I told them how much I enjoyed their repartee, and as I shook hands with Lisa, I thought, *Wow. Look at this stunning woman Dennis married*. I don't claim to know her well, but I've seldom met anyone who exuded such warmth.

Dennis and I entered into a lively exchange while playing *Words with Friends*. He was good, and beat me soundly most of the time, which – to be honest – made me angry now and then. Competitive people love games and hate to lose, but maturity made that a non-issue. My good-humor resurfaced quickly, and I was ready for a re-match.

My "rematch" with Dennis and his death so shortly thereafter has made me think about things, bring things into focus. In our last years what opportunities do we have? We have the opportunity to pay attention, to reconnect with people. We have the opportunity, if we take it, to reconnect with family. Most important of all, we can teach our children two last things.

First, we can demonstrate that life isn't over until the fat lady sings (even if I now consider myself the Singing Fat Lady). Speaking for myself, I can still hope for good news right around the corner, still stand in wonder every time the sun comes up. I can still appreciate the changing seasons with the variety that brings to life on earth. I can still read good books, eat tasty food, enjoy a few pulls on a slot machine hoping every time that I'll win, and win big.

My kids are watching me, even if they don't realize it, as I continued to watch my own mother, and my husband's parents, too. Children, even when they're grown, look to their parents for how to be, yet of all the passages in life, getting old has been the most difficult for me, perhaps because of the disconnect between how my heart and mind feel, which is like they always felt, and how my body feels. My body hurts. Not severely, but chronically. Then there's my place in my own culture. As far as my culture, I'm quite invisible to anyone who isn't my age, with the exception of my son and my daughter.

I'm not doing too well at aging, but I'm trying to avoid becoming what I dislike in other seniors. I don't complain about my aches and pains constantly. I cultivate new interests and try to stay aware in a world that's obviously going to hell in a handcart, and when I think that, I remind myself that people my age always think that. I rail about the lack of good manners and modesty on the part of young people, but again, I suspect the older generation has always thought that about the younger one.

In other words, I can show my children how to get old, and didn't Dennis do that well? I hardly knew he was sick until I knew he was dying, because in the simplest terms, he didn't want to talk about it. He wanted to be witty and sharp, ironic and aware, and most of all, alive. Time enough to be sick, when there's no more choice.

I learned more about Dennis Black through the course of his illness. I learned he had an ex-wife he stayed on friendly terms with, and that's not always easy. So well done, Dennis. I learned he had a son with his ex-wife, and he had two sons with Lisa, and the family blended well, the brothers seemed to share great affection. Again, that's not always the case. So well done, Dennis, and Lisa.

The last thing we have to show our children is how to die. I wasn't there, but thanks to Lisa's careful journaling in Caring Bridge, I think

Dennis found contentment at home, and I think he knew when it was time to let go. And that's very well done, Dennis.

And well done, Lisa, for keeping us informed gently and with as much optimism as possible. I understood the situation because I'd been through it with my mother. Diagnosis, surgery, chemo. Then hospice. Someone brings you morphine to keep on stand-by, then when death occurs the hospice person goes to the refrigerator and pours the morphine down the drain before they even check the pulse of the deceased. Probably not a bad idea. I might have ingested it myself as a buffer for dealing with what had just occurred.

In tributes to Dennis after he died I learned he was well-respected within an extremely caring community of journalists and former colleagues. I learned I wasn't the only one who considered him one of the wittiest people I ever knew. Well done, Dennis.

My mother the Butterfly always had courage, and like Dennis, she faced her own death with *joi de vivre*, which in the literal translation means Joy of Life. During her last spring, she wanted to see the celebrated cherry blossoms here in D.C., so we went to the tidal basin. The sun was out, a slight breeze shook bits of blossom onto my dog's shiny black coat, and we picked petals off the bread as we ate our picnic lunch. I'll remember the joy on my mother's face until my own dying day. I thought, *yes, that's how to do it.* She had refused further chemo by then, so she could feel well enough to enjoy the few weeks she had left. Well done, mom. I think Dennis found pleasure in his last days, so well done, Dennis.

I wanted to preserve the cherry blossom moment, so I lined up a photograph, my loved ones in the foreground, the cherry trees and the tidal basin in the background. The camera failed; I had forgotten to change the battery. I understand now it's better that way, for life is ephemeral like the blossoms, and not static like a photo that could never match the memory of that day.

208. Dennis Black, 1946-2016

The two characteristics I admire most in other human beings are courage and a sense of humor, and Dennis had both. He chose to be braver and funnier as time passed, appreciating and facing square the inevitable end to it all, and daring to laugh at the total preposterousness of almost everything. And if you don't believe that, I'll point out that Green Gary, Dennis' funky, five-inch tall, clay alter-ego, was included in the funeral, probably at Dennis' request.

The Class of '64 has lost too many of our number, and I wish I knew enough about each one to have something honest to say, but I don't, and it makes me grateful that at least I came to be better acquainted with Dennis, purely by chance and the easy communication of the internet age.

Death always wins and laughs when we cower on the brink. Dennis stood up straight and cracked wise, so even though death had the last word, I like to think witty Dennis had the last laugh. He showed those who loved him how to get old and keep that sense of humor, and how to die with grace and courage.

So see ya, Dennis, and well done.

CHAPTER TWENTY-ONE

The Rebirth of the Class of 1964

Goodbyes should be short and sweet, and that's how I hope to end *Tuesday in Texas*.

I've revisited a place that will always be dear to me, and a time before everything changed. I've made new friendships and renewed old ones. I've paid homage to what Texas City suffered, and to my mother, my aunts, and other loved ones. I've offered this as a gift to the Class of 1964, a gift that's been accepted with love, which reaffirms that the greatest gains come from giving.

I wanted to include all our class photos, but pictures of large groups are not great at best, unrecognizable at worst, especially when reduced to fit a small page. Instead, I've split both the Fry Group and the Blocker group into two photos. This was easier when I realized that scoundrel Inky Incalcaterra is in both Blocker and Fry photos, so I could cut him out of Blocker and not feel bad about it.

I'll be as brief as I can, but I can't say goodbye without a few words of parting and thanks.

What's the magic of the class of 1964? I've given a good deal of thought to the matter. All graduating classes are special in their own way, but in the case of our class, it's about the timing.

209. Blocker Jr. High Group, Part 1 and 2, TCHS 50th Reunion, Oct 11, 2014.

We graduate and go into the world to build a family, gather material things, rack up accomplishments, watch our world expand, but the years pass and then comes a turning point. Instead of building, we're taking apart, downsizing, moving away, selling off, ungathering. We hardly notice at first, but we have a baby and know it's the last one. We send a son off to college and know the daughter will go soon, and eagerly. We see new families form around our children as our own dissolves, becomes smaller in the place where we live. It's the right and joyful thing, but even so, we're moving toward a final ending.

For us, born in the middle of the last century, it's the season of saying goodbye. This week I closed the door for the last time at a place on the Isle of Palms, South Carolina, a place my husband and I have loved for 21 years, a place we've shared with children, parents, in-laws, friends, cousins, and even a couple of good dogs now gone to heaven. Goodbye to watching the sun rise over the ocean and the warm feeling when I woke up knowing our loved ones were sleeping in the other bedrooms.

210. Girard McKilroy

The beach erosion is troubling. The last major hurricane, Hurricane Hugo, hit the island in 1989, so that part of the coast is overdue. Owning property out-of-state has vexations. But what it comes down to is simple. We sold it because it was time.

Here's part of what our classmate Girard McKelroy said about closing his family home in Texas City. I couldn't say it better, and it's how I feel about leaving the Isle of Palms:

And now the house is gone, and the key that's been on my keychain for decades is gone too. Passages...

211. Levi Fry Jr. High Group, Part 1 and 2, 50th Reunion, Oct. 11, 2014.

I look up words because I love precise definitions, and *passage* is a great word. It's defined as a way through, a change of place or condition, and the process of time passing. And so I placed the extra keys to Summerhouse 311 into the small cabinet by the door, safe there for the new owners. I hope they love it as we have.

There's plenty of life left in our years, but we are moving through, changing places, watching time pass. The greater portion of our lives is behind us, and the losses become impossible to ignore, the loss of physical strength, the compromised vision and hearing, the energy that used to last as long as we needed it now lasts until mid-afternoon. On a good day. The list of things we can no longer do gets longer.

These losses are nothing, though, compared to the loss of those we love. Our parents, siblings, cousins and uncles. The fabulous aunts, if you're lucky enough to have them, all gone now. We live, and joyfully, but the shadow remains, the inevitability of future losses. Unacceptable losses, yet we must accept them, because the bell tolls for us all.

And now the good news.

Our class reunions in earlier years, at least the ones I attended, have always been exceptional in the devotion and care taken by the planners. I had fun and was glad to be there, but reunions when you're still plagued by the insecurities of youth tend to be more about making an impression than making memories. Years passed, and that changed.

As we eased into a time of endings, losses, and goodbyes, somewhere around the 40th reunion, the leadership of the Class of '64 started in on us, sending out announcements and warnings, determined to get our attention, to encourage us, make us understand we were welcome and wanted.

So come and remember. Come and make new memories. Come home. Come back to 1964.

These good people opened our hearts and led us back to Texas City like it was Brigadoon. Do you know the Legend of Brigadoon? It's the story of a mythical village that was cast under a spell and became invisible to the outside world, except for one day every 100 years. It's like our class went its way for so many years (though short of 100 – so far), and then, when the time was right, came palpably alive again, to dance and talk, flirt a little, laugh out loud, see wonder in faces we came close to forgetting. We became as we were in 1964, yet we kept the changes, the wisdom and tolerance, like a symbiotic melding of then and now. Some might call it magic.

At a time of mounting losses, we gained something, a resurrection of the spirit of 1964. By the time of our 60th birthday party, events gained momentum, participation increased. By the 45th reunion and the 50th, we awaited each contact eagerly, knowing we were going to a place that's waxing instead of waning. No one gives a Texas hoot about the extra pounds, the bald heads, the momentary peering at name tags, the peering that leads to "Oh my God! It's you! I'm so happy to see you!" Who cares about anything but being together? Again. A gain.

Because of the wildly successful reunions, no matter what happens next, with the help of pivotal classmates and social media, we'll go on. We'll share grandkids and vacations, life events, pictures of our pets, and we'll mourn together when we say goodbye to another member of our class. We don't have to wonder *whatever happened to...* because we'll know.

Alanis Morissette said "My main objective with every album is to capture a moment in time . . ."

I hope I've captured a few moments in this album, my personal memoir. I know it's been among the most satisfying things I've ever done, and it never would have existed except for the revival of the Class of 1964. Your gift to me has been your enthusiasm, and your willingness to look back with me. I loved writing it, and you've let me know you loved reading it.

So goodbye to *Tuesday in Texas*, with thanks beyond measuring to all of you.

ACKNOWLEDGEMENTS

With Gratitude . . .

I've had so much support and cooperation in writing this memoir, I hardly know where to begin, but special thanks to Al Mitchell, whose photos provided the rich background of our hometown as it was. Not only did he allow me to use photos from his book, *Images of America – Texas City* (available from *Amazon.com*), but he dug through his archives time and again as something I wrote reminded him of an old photograph, which he sent along to me.

Thanks to Leslie Leonard, a talented young artist, for helping me with the final technicalities of formatting a book for print, which was made especially difficult because of all the pictures. Without her, I'm not sure I would have made it over the last hump to publication.

Thanks also to Leslie for turning the photograph of my childhood friend Danise Louise Miller (Cooper) into a beautiful cover, a dreamy representation of every-girl-of-the-time.

Thanks to my daughter Shannon Hayden, who read *Tuesday in Texas* over and over again for errors in syntax and grammar, to the point she probably can recite whole passages by heart.

Thanks to Brian, my husband. While I was head-down and buried in writing, he was doing everything else. Without him, we both would have starved, lived our lives in dirty clothes, and our dog Gatsby would have died from lack of exercise, food, or water.

In the last chapter, I acknowledged how much the support of the Class of '64 sustained and inspired me. And here begins the list of individuals to whom our whole class owes a debt.

First among equals, Judy and Dolores, who between them contributed so much to the resurrection of the spirit of the Texas City High School Class of 1964.

212. Dolores Geaslin and Judy Holcomb, our once and future and always perfect queens!

Thanks to Judy Holcomb, the keeper of the keys, the person I've peppered with questions, the person who lets us know of events and passages, and GOTCHA Queen for the past three years. (GOTCHA, for those who may not know, is Girls of Texas City High Alumni.)

Exceptional thanks, also, to Dolores Geaslin, for being Queen of the GOTCHA girls for eight years! Whew. That took courage (smile).

I can't shout out loud enough in appreciation for the 50th Reunion Committee. John Bethscheider, Joycelynn Grigson, Doug Christy (Donna's husband), Judy Holcomb, Donna Cochran, Sandy McWhiter, Dolores Geaslin, Raymond McNeel, Margaret Walker, Roger Bradley, Ruth Loya, Lila Ziegelmeyer, Carolyn Stork, Lewis Sholmire, Peggy Fosdick, Linda Cooper, Richard Steed, Jan Hunter, Charles Elfstrom,

Alice Bucklew, Lana Huestedde, James "Inky" Incalcaterra. The guy under the balloons is PeeWee Bowen, our entertainer and "honorary" class member, who plays at many reunions and says our class is the best!

213. The people who made it happen, our 50th Reunion Committee.

Here's a list given to me by others or lifted from the reunion pamphlets as instrumental in bringing us together. It's alphabetical, and the women are listed by the name they had as our classmates. I apologize for omissions or misspellings.

Joe Amato, John Bethscheider, Roger Bradley, Alice Bucklew, and Donna Cochran. Linda Cooper, Jon Crenshaw, Judy Davis, Charles Elfstrom, and Peggy Fosdick.

Joycelynn Grigson, Jan Hunter, Lana Huestedde, James Incalcaterra, and Richard Jones. David Latimer, Ruth Loya, Raymond McNeel, Sandy McWhirter, and Lewis Sholmire.

Carolyn Stork, Eddie Thompson, Margaret Walker, and Lila Ziegelmeyer.

ABOUT THE AUTHOR

Singapore 2014.

Rebecca Long Hayden grew up in Texas City and went to work for NASA at Clearlake after graduation in 1964. Her career in government led to employment with NASA, the U.S. Air Force, the Centers for Disease Control and Prevention, and the U.S. Department of State.

She's a published author of short stories, non-fiction articles, and even a few movie reviews.

After living and working in nine states and two foreign countries, she presently lives in Northern Virginia with her husband of 45 years, Brian Hayden. She continues to read, write, and enjoy her daughter Shannon, and her son Sam, his wife Amy, their three sons Cody, Austin, and Wyatt.

Her e-mail address is tuesdayintexas@gmail.com.